# WORD FROM

# A SOLDIER

*A 2005 Wartime
Deployment Devotional*

by Eric E. Scheidt, Sr.

Traitmarker Books | Franklin, TN

*Published by TRAiTMARKER BOOKS*
*traitmarkerbooks.com*
*traitmarker@gmail.com*

*Printed in the United States of America*

## ACCLAIM FOR
## WORD FROM A SOLDIER

### ★★★★★

*"An encouraging read that is a reminder that everywhere
we go and in all we do, God is there waging the battles
for us and with us."*

*"This read is a peaceful place to come when we need
reminder that God is with us in the depths of war.
When chaos is overwhelming us God breaches
the catastrophe and calms our soul."*

*"I have thoroughly enjoyed reading the Word From a
Soldier. It is not just for soldiers, but for anyone looking to
deepen their walk with Christ through
biblical insight and teaching."*

*"Eric has a unique way of finding the everyday life
application in Scripture. His love of God and passion for
discipleship come through in his collection of devotions."*

*" I love these devotionals... It is refreshing to experience a
'boots on the ground' perspective of God's love and leading
throughout challenging and sometimes hostile
environments."*

*This is written first and foremost for my Lord and Savior Jesus Christ, for without Him none of this would be possible. Secondly, I dedicate this to my Grandpa and Grandma Scheidt. They were the epitome of what love of God and family are all about. Finally, I dedicate this to my wife, Michelle, who has stuck with me through all these years. Thank you for believing in me and standing beside me through it all.*

# TABLE OF CONTENTS

Sat 01-Jan-05
    NEWS OF THE DAY

Sun 02-Jan-05
    NEWS OF THE DAY

Mon 03-Jan-05
    NEWS OF THE DAY

Tue 04-Jan-05
    NEWS OF THE DAY

Wed 05-Jan-05
    NEWS OF THE DAY

Thu 06-Jan-05

Fri 07-Jan-05

Sat 08-Jan-05
    NEWS OF THE DAY

Sun 09-Jan-05

Mon 10-Jan-05
NEWS OF THE DAY

Tue 11-Jan-05
NEWS OF THE DAY

Wed 12-Jan-05
NEWS OF THE DAY

Thu 13-Jan-05

Fri 14-Jan-05

Sat 15-Jan-05

Sun 16-Jan-05
NEWS OF THE DAY

Tue 18-Jan-05

Wed 19-Jan-05
NEWS OF THE DAY

Thu 20-Jan-05

Fri 21-Jan-05
NEWS OF THE DAY

Sat 22-Jan-05

Sun 23-Jan-05
NEWS OF THE DAY

Mon 24-Jan-05
    NEWS OF THE DAY

Wed 26-Jan-05
    NEWS OF THE DAY

Thu 27-Jan-05
    NEWS OF THE DAY

Fri 28-Jan-05
    NEWS OF THE DAY

Sat 29-Jan-05
    NEWS OF THE DAY

Sun 30-Jan-05
    NEWS OF THE DAY

Mon 31-Jan-05

## FEBRUARY                                53-84

Tue 01-Feb-05

Wed 02-Feb-05

Thu 03-Feb-05
    NEWS OF THE DAY

Fri 04-Feb-05

Sat 05-Feb-05

Sun 06-Feb-05

Mon 07-Feb-05
    NEWS OF THE DAY

Tue 08-Feb-05

Wed 09-Feb-05

Thu 10-Feb-05

Fri 11-Feb-05
    NEWS OF THE DAY

Sat 12-Feb-05

Mon 14-Feb-05

Tue 15-Feb-05

Wed 16-Feb-05

Thu 17-Feb-05
    NEWS OF THE DAY

Fri 18-Feb-05
    NEWS OF THE DAY

Sat 19-Feb-05
    NEWS OF THE DAY

Sun 20-Feb-05

Mon 21-Feb-05

Tue 22-Feb-05

NEWS OF THE DAY

Wed 23-Feb-05

Thu 24-Feb-05

Fri 25-Feb-05

Sun 27-Feb-05

Mon 28-Feb-05

NEWS OF THE DAY

## MARCH                                    85-122

Tue 01-Mar-05

Wed 02-Mar-05
NEWS OF THE DAY

Thur 03-Mar-05
NEWS OF THE DAY

Fri 04-Mar-05

Sun 06-Mar-05

Mon 07-Mar-05
NEWS OF THE DAY

Tue 08-Mar-05
NEWS OF THE DAY

Wed 09-Mar-05

NEWS OF THE DAY

Thu 10-Mar-05
NEWS OF THE DAY

Fri 11-Mar-05

Sat 12-Mar-05

Sun 13-Mar-05

Mon 14-Mar-05
NEWS OF THE DAY

Tue 15-Mar-05
NEWS OF THE DAY

Wed 16-Mar-05

Thur 17-Mar-05

Fri 18-Mar-05

Sat 19-Mar-05

Sun 20-Mar-05
NEWS OF THE DAY

Mon 21-Mar-05
NEWS OF THE DAY

Wed 23-Mar-05

Thu 24-Mar-05
NEWS OF THE DAY

Fri 25-Mar-05

Sat 26-Mar-05

Sun 27-Mar-05

Mon 28-Mar-05

Tue 29-Mar-05

Sun 30-Mar-05

Thu 31-Mar-05

    NEWS OF THE DAY

**APRIL & MAY**          123-166

Fri 01-Apr-05

Sat 02-Apr-05
    NEWS OF THE DAY

Sun 03-Apr-05
    NEWS OF THE DAY

Mon 04-Apr-05

Tue 05-Apr-05

Wed 06-Apr-05

Thu 07-Apr-05

Fri 08-Apr-05

NEWS OF THE DAY

Sat 09-Apr-05
NEWS OF THE DAY

Sun 10-Apr-05

Mon 11-Apr-05

Tue 12-Apr-05

Wed 13-Apr-05

Thu 14-Apr-05
NEWS OF THE DAY

Fri 15-Apr-05

Mon 09-May-05

Tue 10-May-05
NEWS OF THE DAY

Wed 11-May-05
NEWS OF THE DAY

Thu 12-May-05
NEWS OF THE DAY

Fri 13-May-05
NEWS OF THE DAY

Sat 14-May-05

Sun 15-May-05

Mon 16-May-05
NEWS OF THE DAY

Tue 17-May-05
NEWS OF THE DAY

Wed 18-May-05

Thu 19-May-05

Fri 20-May-05

Sat 21-May-05

Tue 24-May-05

Wed 25-May-05
NEWS OF THE DAY

Thu 26-May-05
NEWS OF THE DAY

Fri 27-May-05

Sat 28-May-05
NEWS OF THE DAY

Sun 29-May-05

Tue 31-May-05

**JUNE**

Wed 01-Jun-05 08:27

Thu 02-Jun-05 09:21
    NEWS OF THE DAY

Fri 03-Jun-05 10:13

Sat 04-Jun-05 09:21

Sun 05-Jun-05 11:26

Mon 06-Jun-05 09:16

Tue 07-Jun-05 11:31
    NEWS OF THE DAY

Wed 08-Jun-05 08:43

Thu 09-Jun-05 09:28
    NEWS OF THE DAY

Fri 10-Jun-05 10:00

Sat 11-Jun-05 08:43

Sun 12-Jun-05 08:41

Mon 13-Jun-05 09:00
    NEWS OF THE DAY

Tue 14-Jun-05 09:11

Thu 16-Jun-05 10:34
    NEWS OF THE DAY

Fri 17-Jun-05 09:35

NEWS OF THE DAY

Sat 18-Jun-05 09:23
 NEWS OF THE DAY

Sun 19-Jun-05 10:25

Tue 21-Jun-05 09:01

Thu 23-Jun-05 09:00
 NEWS OF THE DAY

Fri 24-Jun-05 11:20

Sat 25-Jun-05 08:38

Mon 27-Jun-05 10:28
 NEWS OF THE DAY

Tue 28-Jun-05 09:09

Wed 29-Jun-05 09:45

Thu 30-Jun-05 07:39

 NEWS OF THE DAY

## JULY & AUGUST                    201-238

Sat 02-Jul-05 10:21
 NEWS OF THE DAY

Mon 04-Jul-05 09:17
 NEWS OF THE DAY

Tue 05-Jul-05 09:48
    NEWS OF THE DAY

Wed 06-Jul-05 09:46
    NEWS OF THE DAY

Thu 07-Jul-05 11:08
    NEWS OF THE DAY

Fri 08-Jul-05 09:35
    NEWS OF THE DAY

Sun 10-Jul-05 10:08
    NEWS OF THE DAY

Mon 11-Jul-05 09:54
    NEWS OF THE DAY

Tue 12-Jul-05 10:09
    NEWS OF THE DAY

Wed 13-Jul-05 09:16
    NEWS OF THE DAY

Thu 14-Jul-05 09:34
    NEWS OF THE DAY

Fri 15-Jul-05 09:43
    NEWS OF THE DAY

Sun 17-Jul-05 11:04
    NEWS OF THE DAY

# FOREWORD

I met Eric Scheidt in the early part of 2018 through a Bible study at a local gun store where veterans fellowshipped, studied, and worshiped together. In the year and a half since I had bought a house, I hadn't really connected with any local veterans. Eric immediately struck me as a man with a mission to share his love and connection to God with others. Eric told me about his time in combat, the writing of his monthly devotional while in country and the extensive email list he compiled for distributing it. His desire was to rekindle his newsletter in the United States.

I served a combined twenty-eight months over two deployments in a combat zone. During my first deployment to Iraq, I ended up in areas where God and His people had walked together: the remnants of the Walls of Jericho, Babylon where the Daniel the prophet served King Nebuchadnezzar and then ended up in a den of lions. I focused my attention on my relationship during that deployment. Feeling His presence there was amazing.

Having spent a lot of time post-combat integrating my faith journey into every aspect of my own healing like my books, workshops, music, farm and nonprofit, I have an intense respect for how much Eric desires to help his fellow veterans and their families grow in their faith. Veterans by the thousands are turning to their faith in God as a way to navigate the effects of coming home after war. Of the many who I know, Eric is one veteran who has the strongest drive to see other veterans develop a deeper walk with Jesus.

Eric's devotional is a real-world, no-nonsense approach to developing a study and worship of God. I pray that you enjoy and grow in your journey while using Eric's devotional as a guide on that path.

Malachias Gaskin | *A Warrior's Garden*
Sgt. U.S. Army (Ret.)

# A Note from the Publisher

When Eric first explained to me the 2005 origin story of this project, he described it as a way for him to keep rooted in his faith amid the chaos, imminent danger and unexpected circumstances to which combat & support personnel are subject. A humble pastoral soul, Eric found a way while deployed to Iraq to calm his nerves, keep his mission in perspective and manage his natural concerns for both his immediate and church family.

Eric did this by *serving* on both homefronts. By fulfilling the unofficial role of a chaplain's assistant abroad and by devoting his free time to creating a newsletter of devotional encouragement for his growing email list back home, Eric embodied the role of servant-leader, The copy of *Word from a Soldier* that you hold in your hands is a testament to his Scriptural and emotional reflections fourteen years ago.

*Word from a Soldier* spans eight months of deployment: January 2005-August 2005. Each entry begins with a Scriptural reading and short commentary thereafter: the >word< for the day.

Most entries have a >news of the day< that offers a glimpse of the chaos in country during that time. In my opinion, the >news of the day< makes Eric's entries that much more meaningful.

At the end of each month is a >field notes< section for journaling. I recommend that you use it to record your own thoughts as you read through this journal.

Ultimately, *Word from a Soldier* is a template of how one individual chose to process events outside his control and how he turned that time into a spiritual practice of developing his relationship with God.

As the publisher of this wartime journal, I hope that you find within these pages a similar zeal to develop your inner life in a way that benefits others.

Robbie Grayson | The Publisher

# January 2005

# Sat 01-Jan-05

Proverbs 1:10
*My son, if sinners entice thee, consent thou not.*

The way of the world is so much easier. Every day there are many things that we could do to succumb to the world. Sin is rampant. We must remain strong. We must fill our mind with things from above. Whatever is holy, pure and righteous...we must think on these things.

Lord, as we strive to be more like Jesus let us dwell on heavenly things and not on worldly things.

---

### NEWS OF THE DAY
Sat 01-Jan-05

*SULAIMANIYAH, Iraq -- A suicide car bomber struck a bus carrying Iraqi national guardsmen north of Baghdad yesterday, killing 26 people and wounding six, as insurgents showed no signs of letting up in their campaign to wreck elections scheduled for the end of the month. In other attacks, four Iraqi policemen were killed and one wounded when their vehicle was ambushed near Samarra, about 60 miles north of Baghdad. In Diyala province in the east the deputy governor, Ali Haddawi, was shot dead.*

# Sun 02-Jan-05

Isaiah 3:11-12
*The lofty looks of man shall be humbled, and the haughtiness of men shall be bowed down, and the Lord alone shall be exalted in that day.*
*For the day of the Lord of host shall be upon every one that is proud and lofty, and upon everyone that is lifted up; and he shall be brought low:*

Humility is not something that comes to us very easy. We all are proud of things that we accomplish and do. This verse is letting us know that we will be humbled. God is the only one that will be exalted. In Ephesians 2:8-9 we are told that it is by grace that we are saved and not of any works that we can do lest we boast. The humility that we feel is brought to us by His glory and majesty. We will meet him face to face. At that time, we will fall down on our faces and cry "Holy, Holy, Holy is the Lord God Almighty". I can't wait for that day to come.

Dear Lord, keep me humble and come quickly.

---

## NEWS OF THE DAY
### Sat 02-Jan-05

*BAGHDAD, Iraq -- On Saturday al-Qaeda in Iraq, the militant group led by Abu Musab al-Zarqawi, released a video of five national guardsmen being shot dead in a street as passers-by stopped to watch. The group said it would kill other Iraqis it accused of collaborating with US forces.*

# Mon 03-Jan-05

Romans 5:6-8
*For when we were yet without strength, in due time Christ died for the ungodly.*
*For scarcely for a righteous man will one die: Yet peradventure for a good man some would even dare to die.*
*But God commendeth his love toward us, in that while we were yet sinners, Christ died for us.*

I was talking with someone the other day and we were talking about how God died for a crummy sinner like me. He didn't wait until I had started doing things right. He didn't wait until I had paid a lot of money. He died for me because I could not do it for myself. So many times, we look at others around us and say I was never like them. I never did this bad thing or was that type of person. The Bible says that there is none righteous no not one. As we look at others we need to realize that our sin was just as great as theirs is. Sin is sin, and Jesus died for it all. He died because no one else could. I just think that it is amazing that He loved me so much that He would

23

die for me: a despicable sinner as I am.

NEWS OF THE DAY
Mon 03-Jan-05

*BAGHDAD, Iraq -- A suicide bomb exploded near the party headquarters of the Iraqi National Accord Party, which is the party of Iraqi interim Prime Minister Ayad Allawi. The explosion killed two police officers and one civilian and injured twenty-five other people. Allawi was not inside the building at the time of the explosion.*

# Tue 04-Jan-05

Proverbs 4:24-27
*Put away from thee a forward mouth, and perverse lips put far from thee.*

*Let thine eyes look right on, and let thine eyelids look straight before thee.*

*Ponder the path of thy feet, and let all thy ways be established.*

*Turn not to the right hand nor to the left: remove thy foot from evil.*

As we live our lives it is so easy to slip up and look toward the left and the right and do what the world wants us to do. I am made very aware of how easy it is when I hear people cuss. I have many times looked left and right and not kept my eyes on Jesus. My desire is to keep my mind on Jesus. When we keep focused on Him it is much easier to stay on the straight and narrow. The straight and narrow is not the easiest road but it is ultimately the only way to keep your feet from sinning.

24

*BAGHDAD, Iraq -- On January 4, the militant group Jaish Ansar al-Sunnah claimed responsibility for yesterday's, attack, citing the upcoming elections as their motivation.*

# Wed 05-Jan-05

Psalm 5:1-3

*Give ear to my words, 0 Lord, consider my meditation.*

*Hearken unto the voice of my cry, my King, and my God: For unto thee will I pray.*

*My voice shalt thou hear in the morning, 0 Lord; in the morning will I direct my prayer unto thee, and will look up.*

When does the Lord hear your voice? Is it in the morning? Is it in the evening? Is it only at meals? The Lord wants to commune with us. He already knows about you but He wants to establish a personal relationship with you. This means that you can talk to Him. You can tell him how you feel. He wants you to cry out to him in sorrow or anger. If you are happy then he wants to know it. If you are sad then let him know about it. The best thing for you to do is just talk with him.

---

NEWS OF THE DAY
Wed 05-Jan-05

*BAQUBAH, Iraq -- A police checkpoint in the Al-Mafraq neighborhood in Baqubah was attacked by a suicide car bomb. Six police officers were killed and thirteen others wounded. The attack was claimed by the group affiliated with Abu Musab al-Zarqawi, Tanzim Qa'idat Al-Jihad fi Bilad al-Rafidayn.*

# Thu 06-Jan-05

1 John 3:13
*Marvel not, my brethren, if the world hate you.*

We are going to be hated. We will be attacked. Sometimes things are going to happen to us and we will not why. We will feel that we are being unjustly treated. These times are going to be trying for you. Have patience. God will help you overcome. I was watching someone eat an "ANISE Cookie" the other day and he didn't like it. He spit it out of his mouth. There are many people of the world that are going to "spit you" out of their lives because you preach the message of life. Many people just don't want to hear about it. They want to fill the void in their life with anything but God. I was talking to a soldier yesterday and we were discussing how people will try to fill the void in their life with drugs, alcohol, sex, kids, marriage, etc. They try to fill it with anything they can except the one true thing that was meant to fill it and that is a personal relationship with Jesus Christ. Do not become upset when you are hated because it is understood that evil will hate good.

# Fri 07-Jan-05

Psalm 7:1
*O Lord my God, in thee do put my trust: save me from all them that persecute me and deliver me.*

The author of this Psalm identifies the Lord as his God. He is making God personal to him.

Only in a personal God can we put our trust. Many of us have made gods out of other things. Our gods could be our new car, our house, our motorcycle, even our family. When we put our trust in these things they will fail. I know that it is so hard sometimes to adjust our thinking and only focus on the Lord and make him our personal God. He is the only one that will save us and deliver us from all the problems that the devil will throw out in our path. Today make the Lord your God and put all of your trust in Him and Him alone.

## Sat 08-Jan-05

Romans 6:1-2

*What shall we say then? Shall we continue in sin, that grace may abound? God forbid. How shall we, that are dead to sin, live any longer therein?*

When we become Christians, we are to put our sins behind us. We should strive to live a blameless life. It is understood that we are going to falter and we will sin, but we are not to sin just because God's grace is sufficient. I was talking with a soldier the other day and he had just gotten saved. He was uneasy because all he wanted to do was get saved and then continue to live his life as he had been before. He said that he didn't want to change. I explained that God will help him change in time. You must be willing to change though. God is not going to force you to change. In Revelation it talks about being either hot or cold. If you are neither then you are distasteful to God and you will be spit out of his mouth. I am not sure that God is speaking in actualities, but I know that He wants us to either be on fire for him or not. We should not ride the fence of the world and continue to dabble in the ways of the world. We need not live in sin any longer.

NEWS OF THE DAY
Sat 08-Jan-05

*FALLUJA, Iraq -- A suicide bomber detonated his vehicle at a gas station in southern Baghdad, near a police checkpoint. Four civilians were killed and nineteen people were wounded in the attack. The station, believed to be the target of the attack, was crowded with people at the time of the attack, due to the fuel shortage. Three cars were also destroyed in the attack.*

# Sun 09-Jan-05

2 Timothy 2:3, 4
*Thou therefore endure hardness as a good soldier of Jesus*
Christ.
*No man that warreth entangleth himself with the affairs of*
*this life; that he may please him who hath chosen him to be a soldier.*

Tents, port-a-johns, foxholes, MREs are all a sign of being a
soldier. They are all hard to deal with at times. What are the signs of
being a Christian? We are His Light in a dark world. How are we to
fight this battle of light against darkness? In this scripture Paul is
telling Timothy that he should not entangle himself with the regular
affairs of this life. We are to strive to live a life pleasing to Christ. As a
soldier I must understand that I can't focus on things that are
happening around me. My goal is to accomplish the mission that my
commander has set before me. The same thing is true in our walk
with Christ. I must not focus on what the world is doing. I must
focus on what my mission is for Christ. As we strive to be a soldier
for Christ we must not look to the left or the right. We have one
mission and one alone. That mission is to be a light in a dark and
dying world. Let us be that light for him today.

# Mon 10-Jan-05

Hebrews 13:7
*Remember them which have the rule over you, who have*
*spoken unto you the word of God: whose faith follow, considering the*
*end of their conversation.*

When was the last time you prayed for your boss? Did you
know that they need to be prayed for as well? When was the last time
you prayed for your pastor? They need prayer too. They go through
the same temptations that we go through. Seldom do we look at our
pastor and notice if they are in need. Most of the time we are
thinking how they take care of my needs today. Take some time today
and pray for your leaders, your spiritual leaders as well as your boss.

Also pray for our president and our Congress. They need prayer as well. We need to lift them up to the throne of grace and petition to God on their behalf. Our president should always be on our prayer list. He is the ultimate leader of our nation and we need to be praying for discernment to be given to him as it was given to King Solomon. Today pray for our leadership.

---

NEWS OF THE DAY
Mon 10-Jan-05

*RUBAI'A, Iraq -- A suicide bomber drove his vehicle into an Iraqi Border Security Forces base in Rubai'a, killing four soldiers and damaging the building.*

# Tue 11-Jan-05

Matthew 14:30-31
*But when he saw the wind boisterous, he was afraid; and beginning to sink, he cried, saying, Lord save me.*
*And immediately Jesus stretched forth his hand, and caught him, and said unto him, O thou of little faith, wherefore didst thou doubt?*

This morning we were awakened by what seemed to be a barrage of either mortars or rockets. My first inclination was to think "Oh that is just one", but they kept happening. I have been praying earnestly that God would place a protective barrier around this base and that the angels would "play baseball" with the in-coming rounds. I began to think that God needed to send those angels back to spring training because there seemed to be a lot of them getting by. I was literally on my face in my trailer calling out to God to keep us safe and secure and to protect us. All went quiet for about 3 hours, then about 0530 this morning the barrage started again.

Only this time the barrage was even closer together. I literally made the decision to go to the bunker. As I went to the bunker I began to look around me and realized that I was the only one that was doing this. There were people doing PT. People were

29

starting to go to work. They were acting like nothing was happening. I thought they were all crazy. Then I stopped someone and asked them what was going on, as calmly as I could. They informed me that it was outgoing rounds. We were testing our guns. What a relief. Here I was worrying that God was not taking care of me and actually He was all along. When I was thinking about this I realized that my faith must grow more. My prayer every day is Lord, I believe. Help thou my unbelief. May that be your prayer today.

---

## NEWS OF THE DAY
### Tue 11-Jan-05

*BASRA, Iraq -- A suicide bomber detonated his vehicle outside the Independent Electoral Commission in Basra, also the location of the Virtuous People Party headquarters. The explosion also occurred near the home of former head of the city's security affairs, Shaykh Hasan al-Qatrani. The explosion damaged the official's home and the commission building, but caused no casualties.*

# Wed 12-Jan-05

Proverbs 12:15
*The way of a fool is right in his own eyes: but he that hearkeneth unto counsel is wise.*

The book of Proverbs has so many great sayings that still apply to today. This verse is so true. I don't know how many times I go through my day and make a hasty decision without thinking it through. When I was young I took a personality test. That test identified me as being impulsive at times. This can be a good characteristic but there are times it can be a negative. If we are to be wise we must be able to listen to others and make decisions on the whole story and not just a portion of it. I would also caution you to seek wise counsel and not just someone who will have the same opinion that you might have just so that you can get someone to agree with you. Being wise is something that we all should want and there are people who are wiser in other areas of life than I am, so I should enlist their input as I would hope that they would enlist my help when they need it.

## Thu 13-Jan-05

Proverbs 13:3

*He that keepeth his mouth keepeth his life: but he that openeth wide his lips shall have destruction.*

Our mouth and tongue are the source of many bad things in our life. During last night's bible study, we discussed that it is much better for us to be quick to listen, slow to speak and slow to become angry. If I can control what comes out of my mouth it is a good thing. So many times we find ourselves saying things we really didn't mean. Instead, we need to always test what we are saying through the Spirit. "Is what I am saying of God and does it really need to be said?" How many times have we seen people must apologize for something that they said inadvertently but they offended someone? We must always put what we are about to say to a test. Is this what Christ would really want us to say? If it isn't then don't say it.

Lord, help us to become better listeners and talk less.

## Fri 14-Jan-05

*Read Acts 26:1-24*

Paul here is telling his life testimony to King Agrippa. He is telling how he was living in sin and how God saved him from the mire of sin and brought him into a new life. Each of us has a story to tell of how God redeemed us out of the pit of hell. So many of us are worried about what other people are going to say if we tell them what God did for us. In verse 24 Festus told Paul that he was mad. Many people will tell us that we are mad as well. The Bible commands us to go into the entire world and tell people the good news about Christ. How will they know if we don't go? My challenge today is to tell someone today what Christ has done for you and how he has changed your life.

# Sat 15-Jan-05

Proverbs 15:1-2
*A soft answer turneth away wrath, but grievous words stir up anger.*
*The tongue of the wise useth knowledge aright: but the mouth of fools poureth out foolishness.*

In our life there are many occasions that we have to be tactful when telling someone something. When I was growing up in my early years of the military, I once had a team chief tell me that I needed to be more tactful when I said things. I would just tell people how I felt, and it didn't matter how I told them. The way I told them showed just how foolish I was. There are many times now that I struggle not to say something until I have tested it against the Spirit. The spirit will make us wise if we ask him to help. Strive to think before you say something today.

# Sun 16-Jan-05

James 1:22-34 (NIV)
*Do not merely listen to the word, and so deceive yourselves. Do what it says.*
*Anyone who listens to the word but does not do what it says is like a man who looks at his face in a mirror*
*and, after looking at himself, goes away and immediately forgets what he looks like.*

This verse has been laid on my heart for a couple of days now. In our Bible study we have been studying the book of James. It was so hard for me to understand this verse until I had someone explain it to me. He said that our mirror is like the church. While we are at church Christ shines through us. What happens when we leave church and others see us? When we walk away others should see Christ in us as well. I thought this was a great point. Do I only allow

Christ to shine when I am around church or other believers? I shouldn't be just a Sunday morning Christian. How many people see Christ in You? Lord, may we be a light for You today. May those around us see Christ in our everyday life and not just when we stand in front of the mirror.

---

NEWS OF THE DAY
Sun 16-Jan-05

*KUT, Iraq -- A suicide bomber detonated his vehicle in a crowd of people gathered for the funeral procession of a police officer. Seven civilians and the bomber were killed in the attack. The incident occurred near Kut.*

# Tue 18-Jan-05

1 Corinthians 12:14
*For the body is not one member, but many.*

There are so many people that think that they are the most important thing in the world. They think that they don't need anyone else. It is all about them. The Church should not be that way. We should all work together for a common good. When we work together we utilize all of our talents and put them together to be used for the common good. Too many people even in the Church just want to do things by themselves. They don't understand that God created us different for a reason. When we work together we become a team united in one cause. That cause should be the salvation of the world.

# Wed 19-Jan-05

Psalm 19:14
*Let the words of my mouth, and the meditation of my heart, be acceptable in thy sight, 0 Lord, my strength, and my redeemer.*

What are the main things people think about in this day

and age? Money, Power, Sex. We all look at what will make us "feel" better. Why is this? We all have a void in our lives that has to be filled by something. God wants to fill that void. He says in Revelation "Behold I stand at the door and knock. If anyone hears my voice and open I will come in and sup with him." God wants to fill that void. We need to let him monitor the meditations of our heart. We also must let him screen what we are going to say. I once heard it said that if you wouldn't say that in front of your mother or grandmother then you shouldn't say it. I think that if we wouldn't say it in front of our GOD then we shouldn't say it. If our meditations are where they should be then we won't let anything unwholesome come out of our mouths anyway. We must rely on God to be our strength. He will help us if we just ask him to. LORD, help me to meditate on you more today, than I did yesterday.

---

### NEWS OF THE DAY
Wed 19-Jan-05

*BAGHDAD, Iraq -- Four suicide bombers struck in Baghdad within a 90-minute period, killing at least 25 Iraqis. The targets included the Australian embassy, a hospital, Baghdad International Airport, and the Iraqi army base of Al-Muthana airport. None of the bombers penetrated the security checkpoints at their targets.*

# Thu 20-Jan-05

Isaiah 59:1-2
*Behold, the Lord's hand is not shortened, that it cannot save; neither his ear heavy, that it cannot hear;*
*But your iniquities have separated between you and your God, and your sins have hid his face from you, that he will not hear.*

No matter what sins that you have done, you can be forgiven. Just as Peter lost faith and Jesus had to save him as he was sinking in the water, God is there to lift us up out of our mire of sin. All we must do is repent and turn to Jesus and He will forgive. Even if we are so heavy laden with sin He is there to take that burden off us and give freedom. Freedom is awesome. Our God provides true freedom. Freedom from all worries and pain. I am serving in a country where there are people that don't want others to be free. I am here to try to provide some resemblance of freedom for them. Those people still are not truly free. The Bible says in John 8:36 "If the Son therefore shall make you free, ye shall be free indeed." This is the freedom that we all need to have. It all begins with a personal relationship with Jesus. If you have not done that then you will not have the freedom that He provides. Won't you do that today?

## Fri 21-Jan-05

Jonah 1:1-3

*Now the word of the Lord came unto Jonah the son of Amittai, saying,*

*Arise, go to Nineveh, that great city, and cry against it; for their wickedness is come up before me.*

*But Jonah rose up to fell unto Tarshish from the presence of the Lord, and went down to*

*Joppa; and found a ship going to Tarshish: so he paid the fare thereof, and went down into it, to go with them unto Tarshish from the presence of the Lord.*

Jonah was a man of God. He was one of God's prophets. Even though he was a man of God he still ran from God. In Genesis, the Bible talks about how Adam and Eve hid themselves from God when they sinned. It is amazing how people even today still try to hide from God. We try to hide the sins that we have committed. We try to run from God because we don't want to do what He told us to do. Children sometimes hide from their parents when they have done something wrong. And when their dad or mother finds them, they are kicking and screaming as they are dragged to where they were supposed to be. God doesn't do that to us. He will give us time alone. Sometimes it will take time in a great big fish to get us back on the right track. Sometimes it may take a still small voice. Other times it may take a giant army or a war to get you to where God really

35

wants you. What will it take for you to come out of hiding and into accomplishing God's will.

Challenge for the Day: Are you hiding from God? If so why? Don't be surprised if he takes you out of your comfort zone to get you on track with him.

---

NEWS OF THE DAY
Fri 21-Jan-05

*YOUSSIFIYAH, Iraq -- A suicide bomber drove his ambulance into a crowd of Shiites celebrating their wedding near Youssifiyah, south of Baghdad. Twelve people were killed and sixteen wounded in the attack. The bride and groom were not among the victims.*

# Sat 22-Jan-05

1 Peter 1:15-16
*But as he which hath called you is holy, so be ye holy in all manner of conversation;*
*Because it is written, Be ye holy; for I am holy.*

Holiness is a derivative of being holy. To be holy means to be spiritually pure, or perfect; untainted by evil or sin. This is what Peter is talking about here. We are to be holy in all manner of conversation. One of the things that I am striving to do is work on my tongue. I notice that when I work on an area of my life I become very sensitive to when that area is being abused. It is amazing how many times a day I hear a 4-letter explicative being used. Many times, the person doesn't even realize they are using them. When I look back at my life, I realize how I sounded when I would say the same things. This is still an area that needs to be worked on.

Peter is not only talking about cursing here. He writes, "Be holy in all manner... " This includes gossip or degrading someone as well. The old adage "Sticks and stones will break my bones, but words will never hurt me" is false. Our words are many times more hurtful than the sword. They cut deeper than the knife. How can we be holy in our conversation? We must pass what we say through Christ. He is the true holy meter. We are to follow his example and be holy because he is holy.

## Sun 23-Jan-05

Romans 14:13

*Let us not therefore judge one another any more: but judge this rather, that no man put a stumbling block or an occasion to fall in his brother's way.*

There has been great controversy over what Christians should or shouldn't do. Some say that we shouldn't drink alcohol. Others say that the Bible says that it is okay. Some people say it is okay to eat meat where others say we shouldn't. Some say we shouldn't work on Sundays, but others say it is okay. This whole chapter in Romans speaks to this very issue. I think that the most important thing to come from this chapter is this verse. If we cause someone to stumble because of what we are doing, then we should stop doing it. We shouldn't cause our brother to sin. We shouldn't judge others because of what we feel we should do. God is the one who will judge. He is the only one who has the authority to judge us and it will be for eternity.

NEWS OF THE DAY
Sun 23-Jan-05

*AL-HILLAH, Iraq -- A suicide bomber exploded a minivan packed with explosives outside a polling station in Al-Hillah city, south of Baghdad. No one was killed in the incident, but eight Iraqi army personnel who were guarding the center were wounded in the attack, along with one civilian. Ansar al-Sunnah Army claimed responsibility for the attack.*

# Mon 24-Jan-05

Psalm 133:1
*Behold, how good and how pleasant it is for brethren to dwell together in unity!*

Coming from a family of 11 children we knew what this verse meant. It was a blessing when every one of us was at peace with each other. We actually had many days that everything was fine, but it was always a little bit "busy" and at times we got on each other's nerves. This verse is actually talking about brothers in Christ. There are many believers in the world. I have seen controversies in many churches because people have allowed their own personal feelings and preferences get in the way instead of allowing God to speak through the Bible. So many people are turned from Christianity because they don't want to be a part the quarrel. If you read on in chapter 133, the author describes how pleasant it truly is. Lord, may we as Christians truly learn how pleasant it is to be in unity one with another.

---

### NEWS OF THE DAY
Mon 24-Jan-05

*BAGHDAD Iraq -- A suicide bomber detonated his vehicle at a police checkpoint outside the Baghdad party offices of the Iraqi National Accord Party, the party of interim Prime Minister Ayad Allawi. The attack injured at least ten people, including eight policemen and two civilians. Only the bomber was killed in the attack. The group affiliated with Abu Musab al-Zarqawi, Tanzim Qa'idat Al-Jihad fi Bilad al-Rafidayn, claimed responsibility for the attack.*

# Wed 26-Jan-05

Proverbs 3:5-6
*Trust in the Lord with all thine heart; and lean not unto thine own understanding.*

*In all thy ways acknowledge him, and he shall direct thy paths.*

Trust is an extremely hard concept to understand. Very rarely do we ever truly trust another individual. It is very hard to trust someone that we can see. How much harder is it to trust someone that we can't see? In this verse we are told to trust in the Lord with all of our heart, not part of it. That means allowing God to come and take over all of it. You can't try to keep a portion of it for yourself. You must give it all to him. When we lean on our own understanding then we tend to have problems. God will direct our paths if we allow him.

I like to think of it as if I were driving a car. God is in the passenger seat and I tell Him he can tell me where to go, but I am still in control of my life. It is only when I relinquish the control of the wheel and acknowledge His request to drive my life will He be able to direct my path.

Thought for the day: How lost do you want to be before you allow God to take control of your life?

---

NEWS OF THE DAY
Wed 26-Jan-05

*SINJAR, Iraq -- A suicide bomber detonated a tractor bomb outside the Kurdistan Democratic Party office in Sinjar, killing fifteen people and wounding at least thirty. The group affiliated with Abu Musab al-Zarqawi, Tanzim Qa'idat Al-Jihad fi Bilad al-Rafidayn, claimed responsibility for the attack.*

# Thu 27-Jan-05

Proverbs 27:6, 17
*Faithful are the wounds of a friend; but the kisses of an enemy are deceitful.*

*Iron sharpeneth Iron; so a man sharpeneth the countenance of his friend.*

When your life gets in a rut and you just get it going sometimes you need a helpful prod or push from someone. Believers need to hold each other accountable for staying in the Word and living a Godly life. Your enemy wants to see you stay in the rut and not produce for the kingdom. Sometimes it may take your friend to prod at you just to get you on the right track. I think that it is interesting how the Proverbs talks about iron sharpening iron. There are different ways that iron can sharpen iron. When a blacksmith sharpens a sword, he uses a hammer and beats the iron first. Another way to sharpen a knife is by using an iron file. As Christians we need to utilize whatever it takes to mold each other. Even more importantly we need to allow God the freedom to mold us the way that He desires.

---

NEWS OF THE DAY
Thu 27-Jan-05

*BAGHDAD, Iraq -- Insurgents killed nearly a dozen Iraqis and an American marine yesterday and bombed several polling centres in a wave of violence ahead of Sunday's elections. Hundreds of US soldiers from the Louisiana national guard were deployed from their base in Baghdad to take up positions around the city in preparation for the vote. Even though commanders have said Iraqi troops will be taking frontline responsibility for security on election day, thousands of US troops will also be deployed at checkpoints and running patrols on the day.*

# Fri 28-Jan-05

Proverbs 28:20, 22
*A faithful man shall abound with blessings: but he what maketh haste to be rich shall not be innocent.*

*He that hasteth to be rich hath an evil eye, and considereth not that poverty shall come upon him.*

I have seen so many "get rich quick schemes" in my short life here on earth. There are the commercials that say if you just do this or that you can be rich like me. You have those that say to put all your money in this stock or that bond and it will gain tremendously. I have seen people that relied on the Stock Market and they are broke today. Here the writer of Proverbs is specifically telling us that if you try to get rich quick that you will not be rich but instead, poor. I have heard pastors tell their parishioners that all they had to do to get rich was to give a lot of money to the church. I don't believe that is what God is talking about. Yes we need to give our tithe. We also should give because we feel God has led us to give. When it comes down to giving to God because we want something in return then we are not giving the right way. We will not be "rich" if we try to get it fast. The way that we are blessed is being faithful in all that we do. This means that we may not be "rich" by the worldly standards but we will be blessed by Godly standards. I would rather be blessed by God than have all the riches in the world, wouldn't you?

NEWS OF THE DAY
Fri 28-Jan-05

*BAGHDAD, Iraq -- A suicide car bomb exploded outside of the al-Dora police station and a power station in southern Baghdad. Six police officers were killed in the attack. Two police officers and two civilians were also injured in the incident.*

## Sat 29-Jan-05

PSALMS 23:1-3
*THE LORD IS MY SHEPHERD; I SHALL NOT WANT.*
*HE MAKETH ME TO LIE DOWN IN GREEN*
*PASTURES: HE LEADETH ME BESIDE STILL WATERS.*
*HE RESTORETH MY SOUL: HE LEADETH ME IN*
*THE PATHS OF RIGHTEOUSNESS FOR HIS NAME'S SAKE.*

Are you tired? Do you feel totally burnt-out? Has battle fatigue set in yet? At the time of this newsletter we are going everywhere in all our gear. We are on heightened alert. All our senses

41

should be working overtime. You are probably going to be tired soon. I know that there are so many soldiers that are on the front lines that are feeling this fatigue.

If the Lord is your shepherd, then he wants to lead you to a place of rest. He will make you lie down in a green pasture. A green pasture is soft and relaxing. He wants to lead you by the still waters. Have you ever gone to a lake and just enjoyed sitting there, not doing anything but watch the water? You don't have to sleep to be rested. A lot of times you need to just take time to spend with him and slow down your busy day. He says that he will restore your soul. He wants to be your shepherd, but he will only do that if you will allow him to. He is not going to force you to let him be your guide. The Bible says in Matthew 11:28, "Come unto me, all ye that labor and are heavy laden, and I will give you rest." We must come to him. He will not give us the rest until we ask for it.

Are you tired? If so ASK HIM today to be your shepherd and he will take you to the green pasture.

---

NEWS OF THE DAY
Sat 29-Jan-05

*KHANAQIN, Iraq -- A suicide bomber wearing a jacket filled with explosives blew himself up near the US-Iraqi Joint Coordination Center in Khanaqin, a Kurdish town near the Iranian border. Three Iraqi soldiers and five Iraqi civilians were killed in the attack. The group affiliated with Abu Musab al-Zarqawi, Tanzim Qa'idat Al-Jihad fi Bilad al-Rafidayn, claimed responsibility for the attack. The attack occurs the day before the elections in Iraq.*

## Sun 30-Jan-05

*Read Exodus 2:1-10*

As I read this story this morning I was encouraged with the message that it brings. Timing is everything to God. Moses was placed in the basket and left to float on the river. Soldiers could have come and taken him or killed him. He could have floated down the river. God had a plan. He knew exactly when the Pharaoh's daughter would come by and find Moses. God has a plan for each of us. He has numbered our steps. His plan will happen in His time not ours. We must be willing to wait on Him and allow Him to lead us. Jeremiah 29:11 says that the Lord knows the plans that he has for us. They are to prosper us and not harm us. It is his plan, but we must live in it. Will you wait on the Lord or are you going to force your will on Him?

---

### NEWS OF THE DAY
Sun 30-Jan-05

*FALLUJA, Iraq -- Millions of Iraqis defied a surge of bombings and suicide attacks yesterday to go to the polls in greater than expected numbers for the first democratic elections for 50 years. The electoral commission's provisional estimate of turnout was 57%. Despite an extraordinary security crackdown in which all cars were banned from the streets and most roads were blocked by soldiers and coils of razor wire, more than 40 Iraqis were killed in attacks. At least nine suicide bombers, most with explosives strapped to their chests, detonated themselves near polling stations in Baghdad. Several other targets were hit by mortars, and explosions echoed across Baghdad throughout the day, but still crowds of Iraqis turned out to vote.*

## Mon 31-Jan-05

Ecclesiastes 2:8-11, 18
*I gathered me also silver and gold, and the peculiar treasure of kings and of the provinces: gat me men singers and women singers, and the delights of the sons of men, as musical instruments, and that of all sorts.*
*So I was great, and increased more than all that were before me in Jerusalem: also my wisdom remained with me.*
*And whatsoever mine eyes desired I kept not from them, I withheld not my heart from any joy; for my heart rejoiced in all my labour: and this was my portion of my labour.*
*Then I looked on all the works that my hands had wrought, and on the labour that I had laboured to do: and, behold, all*

*was vanity and vexation of spirit, and there was no profit under the sun.*

*18. Yea, I hated all my labour which I had taken under the sun: because I should leave it unto the man that shall be after me.*

Americans are so bad about wanting everything. The old adage, "He who has the most toys when he dies, wins" depicts the American way of life. All people try to do is get more things. The writer of Ecclesiastes is so right. When we die we leave everything behind. All we can take with us is our souls and what we did for God. All the money and junk that we got along the way is for nothing. Jesus talked to a young ruler who wanted to know how to get to heaven. Jesus told him that he had to keep all the commandments. When he said that he had done this, Jesus told him that he had to sell all that he had and give everything to the poor. The young man could not do this. He didn't realize that everything that he had was not going to get him anywhere in eternity. We must realize that no matter what we have now we must realize that we can't take any of it with us. Only what we have done for eternity will last. What have you done for eternity today?

# -FIELD NOTES-
## *for Journaling*

# FEBRUARY 2005

# Tue 01-Feb-05

Psalms 150
*Praise ye the Lord. Praise God in his sanctuary; praise him in the firmament of his power.*

*Praise him for his mighty acts: praise him according to his excellent greatness.*

*Praise him with the sound of the trumpet: praise him with the psaltery and harp.*

*Praise him with the timbrel and dance: praise him with stringed instruments and organs.*

*Praise him upon the loud cymbals: praise him upon the high-sounding cymbals.*

*Let everything that hath breath praise the Lord. Praise ye the Lord.*

As this weekend drew to a close I just had to sit in awe as God's hand had been seen in so many ways this weekend. This was the first time in Iraq history that there were free elections held.

People came out in droves. The insurgent's fear tactics did not scare them away from voting. There was some loss of life but God definitely protected. People's prayers were answered.

There is so much to be thankful for. God has allowed us to live another day. I have a roof over my head. I have a wonderful wife. I have two wonderful children. I live in the best country in the World. Most importantly I serve a Risen Savior. Praise Him today.

We must take the time to praise the Lord. It oftentimes is hard to praise the Lord. We normally can't accept praise very well, so it is even harder to give it out. One of the best ways that we can praise Him is by praying the Psalms to Him. That is a start. As you become more comfortable doing that then through your own words praise Him. Before long, it will come natural. All God wants is to hear your love through your praise.

# Wed 02-Feb-05

Exodus 6:1-2
*Then the Lord said unto Moses, Now shalt thou see what I will do to Pharaoh: for with a strong hand shall he let them go and with a strong hand shall he drive them out of his land.*

*And God spake unto Moses, and said unto him, I am the LORD:*

In the preceding chapter Moses asked God why he was sent to free the people of Israel. The Egyptians were working the Israelites harder now than they had been before. The leaders of the Israelites came back to Moses and Aaron and wanted to know why they were bringing all this pain on them.

God's answer was very simply, "I am the LORD." In life we tend to question God as to why things are happening. Sometimes things are very painful. They aren't what we want. We want the easy way out. I think this was what Moses was hoping for. He probably thought that all he would have to do was go to Pharaoh and tell him to let the Israelites go and that God would force him to do it. Instead there was resistance. God uses resistance to build our faith. We are not always going to have the easy road. It will be hard at times. We must just be willing to allow God to be the LORD and follow in His paths. He will lead us into victory.

# Thu 03-Feb-05

1 Peter 2:20-21
*For what glory is it, if, when ye be buffeted for your faults, ye shall take it patiently? But if, when ye do well, and suffer for it, ye take it patiently, this is acceptable to God.*

*For even hereunto were ye called: because Christ also suffered for us, leaving us an example, that ye should follow his steps:*

Sometimes we endure punishment or persecution for the wrong reason. We say that it is because we are believers and that we are receiving it for God's sake, when really it is because we didn't follow all of the procedures for something. The preceding verses in 1 Peter talked about submitting yourselves to the ordinances of man for the Lord's sake. There are times that we don't think things are right. Things might infringe on our "rights". When I am being persecuted it is a lot of times because I have done something wrong and then I am reaping a consequence because of it. We need to be aware of when we are enduring the hardship that is come upon us that it is not always because of Christ but it might be because we didn't submit to those around us when we should have.

Read all of chapter 2. I is quite insightful.

## NEWS OF THE DAY
Thu 03-Feb-05

*BAGHDAD, Iraq -- A suicide car bomber detonated his vehicle near a foreign convoy on Baghdad's airport road. Several vehicles were damaged and a house was also damaged. There were some reports of injuries, but no official numbers were released.*

# Fri 04-Feb-05

Proverbs 4:23
*Keep thy heart with all diligence; for out of it are the issues of life.*

Guard your heart. We must be diligent to guard our hearts. Satan sneaks around like a roaring lion. He wants to attack the unsuspecting. He is intent on finding Christians who are backsliding so that he can ruin their witness. If he can ruin their witness and keep someone else from the saving knowledge of Jesus Christ then he has accomplished his mission. Satan doesn't want us to tell others about Jesus. He is intent on having people live in hell with him. Don't let it be you. You must guard your heart. We must not be consumed with the issues of this world. Make your goal go to "follow after righteousness, godliness, faith, love, patience, meekness" (1 Tim. 6:11). Take heart, God has already won the war. Guard your heart and you will win the daily battles.

## Sat 05-Feb-05

Exodus 13:14
*And it shall be when thy son asketh thee in time to come, saying, What is this? That thou shalt say unto him, By strength of hand the Lord brought us out from Egypt, from the house of bondage:*

The Israelites had just endured all the plagues and then the first Passover feast. Moses was instructing the elders and leaders of the tribes of Israel that they would have this feast of celebration. It would be called the feast of unleavened bread. All of the instructions led up to this verse. Moses is instructing the children of Israel to remember this time. He told them, "Don't ever forget what God has done for you and how he brought you out of the land of Egypt."

We must never forget what God has done for us. As things in our lives happen and God works we need to tell others. More importantly we need to tell our children what God has done for us. If we don't tell them about His grace and mercy, then they will not know. I was once told that Christianity is only one generation from extinction. If we keep to ourselves what God has done and don't tell others, then before long no one will know and our next generation will be lost. We can't allow that to happen. We must continue to pass the message on. Will you?

## Sun 06-Feb-05

*Read Exodus 14-15*

Exodus 15:24
*And the people murmured against Moses, saying, What shall we drink?*

Here the people of God have been brought through a great hardship in their life. God not only brought them out of Egypt, he also brought them through the Red Sea on dry ground. He killed all of the Egyptians that had followed them into the sea and had proven one more time that He was more powerful than the Egyptians. The Israelites worshiped and praised God for taking care of them. Then the Israelites walked 3 days journey and couldn't find any good water. They immediately started to grumble. They totally forgot how to trust God when they were in need.

Instead they were worried about what they didn't have and how Moses was going to provide it for them.

Isn't it that way with us? God will take care of a need in our life and we will praise him. Twenty minutes later when something doesn't seem to be working out we start wondering where God is and why this is not going our way. We look to man to fix our problems and not to God.

James 5:16 says, "The effectual fervent prayer of a righteous man availeth much." We must pray fervently to God. Our faith must be on Him and not on man. May we never forget what God has done for us and how he does take care of us, if we only ask.

## Mon 07-Feb-05

*Read Psalm 56*

Psalm 56:3
*What time I am afraid, I will trust in thee.*

I am the oldest of 11 children. I remember when one of my younger brothers was scared of the dark. We lived in an older house that had a fireplace in each room. At night you could hear the wind come down the chimney and it could be scary. My parents would put newspaper in the chimney to keep the "draft" out. One day my brother was found looking up the chimney and when asked about it he said he was looking for the "Giraffe" that dad was trying to keep out. On a more serious note though, this verse was one that we memorized so that when we were scared of the dark we could say this over and over. I have heard it repeated over and over but I have not really found power in it until I have been put in harm's way.

Here I am in Iraq. We have had rockets fired at us that have missed their mark. We have had IEDs blow up and not injure anyone or do damage to a vehicle. We have had soldiers shot at. It is here where you see soldiers putting their faith in God. Is life so easy back home that we fail to place our trust in Him? What will it take to put America back on her knees? During the days following September 11th, the churches were full of people who were scared. They were putting their trust in God. Where are they now? Life has returned back to normal. We have returned to our normal busy nation. We never have time for Him. When will that change? Take time for Him today before you become afraid. He wants a relationship with you that will last through the good times as well as the times that you are afraid.

---

NEWS OF THE DAY
Mon 07-Feb-05

*MOSUL, Iraq -- Twelve police officers were killed by a suicide bomber who lured them towards him and detonated his explosives outside a police station near Mosul Hospital where the men were waiting to collect their wages. Six officers were also wounded in the attack. This was one of two suicide bombings in Iraq on this day. The group led by Abu Musab al-Zarqawi, Tanzim Qa'idat Al-Jihad fi Bilad al-Rafidayn, claimed responsibility for both attacks.*

## Tue 08-Feb-05

John 21:15-17
*So when they had dined, Jesus saith to Simon Peter, Simon, son of Jonas, lovest thou me? He saith unto him, Yea, Lord; thou knowest that I love thee. He saith unto him, Feed my lambs.*
*He saith to him again the second time, Simon, son of Jonas,*

*lovest thou me? He saith unto him, Yea, Lord; thou knowest that I love thee. He saith unto him, feed my sheep.*

*He saith unto him the third time, Simon, son of Jonas, lovest thou me? Peter was grieved because he said unto him the third time, Lovest thou me? And he said unto him, Lord, thou knowest all things' thou knowest that I love thee. Jesus saith unto him, Feed my sheep.*

When Jesus pulled Peter aside, why do you think He asked Peter this question? He asked the question to make a point to Peter. Peter had returned to fishing after Christ's death.

He thought that God could not use him because he had denied him 3 times when Jesus needed him most. Peter went back to doing his regular occupation. He decided that he was not usable to God any more. In this verse Jesus asked 3 times whether or not Peter loved him. Then the most important words were given. FEED MY SHEEP. Jesus told Peter that He still had a purpose for his life. Even after Peter had done the unthinkable Jesus still wanted to use him.

You know, God is still that way today. No matter what you have done, or where you have been, He still wants to know if you love him. If you do, then he wants to use you to feed his sheep. Take that to heart. Even after Paul had been persecuting Christians, God used him to feed his sheep. It is amazing. God still uses Peter and Paul today to feed the sheep of today.

Will you let him use you?

## Wed 09-Feb-05

1 John 2:15-17
*Love not the world, neither the things that are in the world. If any man love the world. The love of the Father is not in him.*

*For all that is in the world, the lust of the flesh, and the lust of the eyes, and the pride of life, is not of the Father, but is of the world.*

*And the world passeth way, and the lust thereof: but he that doeth the will of God abideth forever.*

Have you ever had a back-seat driver? Isn't that

annoying when they are always telling you what to do and where to go? The god of this world wants to be that back-seat driver. God also wants you to allow Him to be your Co-Pilot. The Devil wants to lead you into a world of lust of the flesh, lust of the eyes and pride of life. God wants to lead you in a life of holiness. The things that the world has to offer look really good right now, but they won't last. What God has to offer will last for all eternity. What direction will you go? Will you go toward God or the world?

You can't have both. We can't serve two masters. Today you must decide which direction you will go.

## Thu 10-Feb-05

Exodus 17:11-12

*And it came to pass, when Moses held up his hand, that Israel prevailed: and when he let down his hand, Amalek prevailed.*

*But Moses' hands were heavy; and they took a stone and put it under him, and he sat theron; and Aaron and Hur stayed up his hands, the other on the other side; and his hands were steady until the going down of the sun.*

In May, my wife and I will have been married for 10 years. During that time we have moved eight times. It is a battle every time to decide how we are going to move. We have always moved ourselves. My wife is a petite 5"1' lady. When we move we don't have anyone else move us. She is my right hand man (woman). We move everything together because we are a team.

This is the way it should be in life. There should never be someone out there all by themselves. When we are battling spiritually it is always best to have two people to lift you up and pray for you as you go through whatever it is that you are battling. Pray for each other. Hold each other accountable for doing the right thing. In doing so, you will win the battle that is waging within.

# Fri 11-Feb-05

*Read Ecclesiastes 3:1-8*

Ecclesiastes 3:3-4
*A time to kill, and a time to heal;
a time to break down, and time to build
up; A time to weep, and a time to laugh; a
time to mourn, and a time to dance;*

Have you ever been just in a funk? Just wanted to bite everyone's head off? I was like that yesterday. I was not even sure why I was that way. I saw it gradually coming on. Some things have been happening here that are just so absurd. I have been very quiet about a lot of my feelings here. I am under the impression that I am here for a year and I will let the "military" mess with me as they will but once I get back then I can do what I need to do to fix some of the issues that I have see. Yesterday evening I went back to my trailer and crawled into bed and went to sleep at 1830. I didn't wake up until 0630 this morning and even then I didn't get up until 0730. was just exhausted. We in the military world could call it Battle Fatigue. I have been working every day since I left over 3 months ago. I have not had a day off. I am exhausted.

When I read this verse, I realized that there is a time for everything. There is a time to break down. There is a time to build up. My verse has been I can do all things through Christ who strengthens me. I agree that this is an important verse. I also have been reading the 23 Psalm that says that the Lord will make us lay down in green pastures. I think that there is a time for us to rest. Today's word is included with a prayer request. That request is that I will not be burnt out; that I will run and not grow weary; that I will finish the fight. Pray that for all the soldiers here as well.

---

NEWS OF THE DAY
Fri 11-Feb-05

*BALAD RUZ, Iraq -- A suicide bomber blew up a car bomb near the a Shiite mosque in Balad Ruz at the end of evening prayers, killing twelve people and wounding twenty-three others. Among those killed were four national guardsmen and eight civilians.*

## Sat 12-Feb-05

Isaiah 40:28-31

*Hast thou not known? Hast thou not heard, that the everlasting God, the Lord, the Creator of the ends of the earth, fainteth not, neither is weary? There is no searching of his understanding.*

*He giveth power to the faint; and to them that have no might he increaseth strength.*

*Even the youths shall faint and be weary, and the young men shall utterly fall:*

*But they that wait upon the Lord shall renew their strength; they shall mount up with wings as eagles; they shall run, and not be weary; and they shall walk, and not faint.*

Our God is a God of strength. He will increase our strength when we rest. He is all powerful. He is the almighty, everlasting Father. He will pick us up when we are tired. It is through him and him alone will we find true strength. At times when we feel that we are going it alone and that we don't see him, it is then when we are being carried by Him.

To all of you out there that prayed and lifted me up yesterday, thank-you. I appreciate the encouraging emails and thoughts that were sent my way. It is so encouraging to know that God has broadened my spiritual family in such a way that it goes from shore to shore. Thank you for allowing God to use you to minister to a lowly soldier here in Iraq. One of my favorite poems is called Footprints. I want to close with that today.

*Footprints in the Sand*

*One night I dreamed I was walking along the beach with the Lord.*
*Many scenes from my life flashed across the sky.*
*In each scene I noticed footprints in the sand.*

63

*Sometimes there were two sets of footprints, other times there was one*
*only.*
*This bothered me because I noticed that during the low periods of my*
*life,*
*when I was suffering from anguish, sorrow or defeat,*
*I could see only one set of footprints, so I said to the Lord,*
*"You promised me Lord, that if I followed you,*
*you would walk with me always.*
*But I have noticed that during the most trying periods of my life*
*there has only been one set of footprints in the sand.*
*Why, when I needed you most, have you not been there for me?" The*
*Lord replied,*
*"The years when you have seen only one set of footprints,*
*my child, is when I carried you."*

Mary Stevens

## Mon 14-Feb-05

Exodus 20:3-5
*Thou shalt have no other gods before me.*

*Thou shalt not make unto thee any graven image, or any*
*likeness of any thing that is in heaven above, or that is in the earth*
*beneath, or that is in the water under the earth:*

*Thou shalt not bow down thyself to them, nor serve them:*
*for I the Lord thy God am a jealous God, visiting the iniquity of the*
*fathers upon the children unto the third and fourth generation of*
*them that hate me.*

It was an extremely emotional day for the Iraqi people
when they tore the statues of Saddam Hussein down. This was a
man who had made them revere him for years. He had placed his
picture up everywhere. There were statues of him everywhere.
Saddam had placed himself way above God.

God is adamant that we place nothing before Him. He
takes three verses here in Exodus 20 to be very specific. He says
that we should not have any other gods before him. Then He

explains exactly what He means. We are not to make any images of anything and worship them. We should not serve them or bow down to them. We should not place anything or anyone above God. If we do there will be serious consequences. God is a jealous God. He doesn't want to share our love with anything or anyone else. We must ensure that we don't let anything get in the way of our love for God. A good test for knowing if we have placed anything above God is to as the following question. "What do I spend most of my time doing?" Is it done for God or is it done to satisfy someone or something else? Have I become my own god because of what I do? If we have taken our focus off of Christ and God then we must refocus on Him and surrender to His will in our life. Only at that time will we be able to truly obey His command of having no other gods before Him.

## Tue 15-Feb-05

Hebrews 10:36
*For ye have need of patience, that, after ye have done the will of God, ye might receive the promise.*

I have been observing a lot of people here recently. Everyone who has been here for a while is starting to grow edgy. Anything gets on their nerves and it becomes a bigger deal than it could be. I am seeing Christian believers bite each other's heads off for the littlest thing. Patience is something that is needed every day. God has a purpose for our life. We must be patient and allow that plan to come about. During the times that we are under a lot of stress and feel that we can't take anything else we need to turn it over to our Lord. There are going to be days that you must turn your load over to the Lord. He says in Matthew 11:28:"Come unto me, all ye that labour and are heavy laden, and I will give you rest." God will give us this promise if we just have the patience to do His will. Sometimes that may mean that we do something that we don't want to do. We might have to do a job that we feel is not ours to do. We need to have to the patience and know that one day we will reap the reward God has promised us. Just be patient!

# Wed 16-Feb-05

Proverbs 16:1-3
*The preparations of the heart in man, and the answer of the tongue, is from the Lord. All the ways of a man are clean in his own eyes; but the Lord weigheth the spirits.*
*Commit thy works unto the Lord, and thy thoughts shall be established.*

Have you ever been told that you did the right thing for the wrong reason? Maybe you were trying to get someone's attention, so you did something good. Verse two tells us that God knows our heart. He knows if we are doing something for the right reason or not. We are told to commit our works to Him. Once we have let Him have control of our life and commit those works to Him then our thought life will be right. If we don't allow God to prepare our hearts and totally clean it, then we will do good things with the wrong intentions in mind.

Allow Him to come in and prepare your heart for His glory.

# Thu 17-Feb-05

Daniel 1:8
*But Daniel purposed in his heart that he would not defile himself with the portion of the king's meat, nor with the wine which he drank: therefore he requested of the prince of the eunuchs that he might not defile himself.*

Daniel had courage. Here he is in a different country. He is a prisoner. He had every right to be scared. He should have done exactly as the king had directed but he had a conviction. Daniel was obedient to the Lord and did as the Lord had directed. He was sure that God would bless him if he did the right thing.

Today we rarely have to worry about our lives being in jeopardy because of our beliefs.

We live in a free society and are allowed to believe as we will. There are people all over the world that are persecuted because of what they believe. In China there are believers that are thrown in prison because of their beliefs. Here in Iraq, people become outcast if they convert to Christianity from a Muslim faith. Their family will disown them. They are courageous though and they will take a stand.

How strong is your faith? Would you die for it? Are you brave enough to take a stand for what who you believe in? Will you stand for Jesus Christ?

---

NEWS OF THE DAY
Thu 17-Feb-05

*BAGHDAD, Iraq -- In Baghdad, a man wearing two suicide vests filled with explosives was shot and killed before he could detonate them.*

# Fri 18-Feb-05

Exodus 32:10-11, 14

*Now therefore let me alone, that my wrath may wax hot against them, and that I may consume them: and I will make of thee a great nation.*

*And Moses besought the Lord his God, and said, Lord, why doth thy wrath wax hot against thy people, which thou hast brought forth out of the land of Egypt with great power, and with a mighty hand?*

*And the Lord repented of the evil which he thought to do unto his people.*

What type of leader was Moses? Remember this is a man that asked God to send someone else to go and. lead the Israelites out of Egypt. He is the same one that said that he couldn't speak.

He told God that he had a stuttering problem. Now he is talking to God and convincing Him that it wouldn't be a good idea to kill all of the Israelites. If you read verses 12 and 13 you will find that Moses lights into God pretty hard about his promises that he has made as well as how God's · reputation was at stake. Today we would say that Moses was pretty blunt with God. He told God how it would be if God went through with His plan to destroy the Israelites. Moses was truly interceding on the Israelites' behalf.

Intercessory prayer is the act of praying for someone else. My pastor was preaching on the types of prayer and he referred to this type of prayer as being the hardest to do. It is extremely hard to take the focus off of me or I and focus on someone else. You will be truly blessed when you can focus on praying for others and not just for your needs alone. It is so much easier to intercede for others though, when your relationship is right with God. If you were a defense attorney and you were in court do you think it would be easier to sway the judge to go lenient on your client if you had a good rapport with the judge? That is the same way it is with intercession. If we are talking to God on a regular basis and our relationship is a personal one then it is much easier to intercede on others behalf.

May you make your relationship with God continue to grow as you seek Him.

---

NEWS OF THE DAY
Fri 18-Feb-05

*BAGHDAD, Iraq -- A suicide bomber detonated himself at an Iraqi police and National Guard checkpoint in a Sunni neighborhood in Baghdad. Two police officers and a national guard member were killed in the attack.*

## Sat 19-Feb-05

Psalm 62:5-7
*My soul, wait thou only upon God; for my expectation is from him.*

*He only is my rock and my salvation: he is my defense; I shall not be moved.*

*In God is my salvation and my glory; the rock of my strength, and my refuge, is in God.*

The Psalms of David are some of the most inspirational chapters in the Bible. David was a man that saw many fearful days. His life was constantly in jeopardy. He was a warrior. He was then hunted by King Saul because he knew that God had picked David to be the next king. David spent many nights either in caves or in fields praying to God to be his comforter. He was asking God to be his protector.

In the Military we have what is called "Cover" and "Concealment". Concealment can hide you but it won't protect you. A round can go right through concealment. Cover on the other hand is protection. We use trees or mounds of dirt for cover. The best thing that we can use is a rock for protection. In this verse we see that God is our rock. He will defend us against what the enemy has to offer. Everything that the devil throws our way has to come through God first. Don't lose heart when your life is in turmoil and it looks like everyone is against you. God is there to be your refuge and defense if you will allow Him to.

---

## NEWS OF THE DAY
### Sat 19-Feb-05

*KARBALA, Iraq -- Five blasts in Iraq, including at least four suicide bombings, killed at least 12 people Saturday as Shiite Muslim worshippers around the country celebrated the holiest day of the year. The attacks came one day after a string of bombings killed at least 36 people. Saturday's attacks, during the religious festival of Ashura, came despite stepped-up security around the country. Authorities had hoped to prevent a repeat of last year's attacks during Ashura, in which insurgents killed at least 181 people in twin blasts in Karbala and Baghdad.*

## Sun 20-Feb-05

Daniel 3:16-18
*Shadrach, Meshach, and Abednego, answered and said to*

69

*the king, 0 Nebuchadnezzar, we are not careful to answer thee in this matter.*

*If it be so, our God whom we serve is able to deliver us from the burning fiery furnace, and he will deliver us out of thine hand, O, king.*

*But if not, be it known unto thee, 0 king, that we will not serve thy gods, nor worship the golden image which thou hast set up.*

These young men had true faith. It was a life or death situation. Bow down before the statue of Nebuchadnezzar or die. These Hebrew servants said that they would not bow down. It is interesting how King Nebuchadnezzar's initial response was. When it had been reported that they would not worship his idol, the king was upset but he gave them a second chance. He was hoping that they would change their minds. These Hebrew boys were good help. They were smart and did things wisely. I don't think that he really wanted to kill them. So he gave them a second chance. The weirdest thing happened. When he gave them a second chance they told him that their God would deliver them from the furnace and even if he didn't they still would not worship the image. This was a true step of faith. What they were saying was that they new that God could save them from the fiery furnace, but it was still up to Him if He would do it. God had the abilities to do it but was it in His will for that to happen.

The world as we know it is starting to change. God is being taken out of schools and out of society. Other "gods" are being pushed on us. Are we going to be like so many other Jews in this story and bow down? Are we going to pretend to worship these other "gods" or are you going to trust our living Savior and Him alone? He will deliver us from this world. But if He chooses to let us stay here longer, then I will still not worship the "gods" of this world.

## Mon 21-Feb-05

2 Peter 3:8-10
*But, beloved, be not ignorant of this one thing, that one day is*

*with the Lord as a thousand years, and a thousand years as one day.*

*The Lord is not slack concerning his promise, as some count slackness; but is longsuffering to us-ward, not willing that any should perish, but that all should come to repentance.*

*But the day of the Lord will come as a thief in the night; in the which the heavens shall pass away with a great noise, and the elements shall melt with fervent heat, the earth also and the works that are therein shall be burned up.*

Edgar Whisenant wrote a book titled "88 Reasons why Christ will Return in 88". In that book he gave reasons why he felt that his theory that Christ was coming back in 1988 was accurate. There were many people that fell for this way of thinking. Many people started to prepare for His return. They waited, and waited. Nothing happened. In today's verse the Bible says that the Day of the Lord will come when no one knows it. It will be like a thief in the night.

When I was a child our house got robbed. We were on vacation. When we got home we noticed that something was wrong and then things went from bad to worse. There were things missing. Now think about that in regards to this verse. First Jesus will come back as a thief in the night. No one will be aware of when He will come. He will steal away those who have repented. So many people who have thought that Christ was coming back sooner have "prepared" for it. What we need to do is live our life everyday following Christ's example. He doesn't want us to prepare for His coming. We will grow tired of waiting. Instead we must live our life always for Him.

Are you ready for His return? Will you be left behind? If you have questions regarding this email me or contact me and we can discuss this in depth.

## Tue 22-Feb-05

Job 1:7-8
*And the Lord said unto Satan, Whence comest thou? Then Satan answered the Lord, and said, From going to and fro in the earth,*

*and from walking up and down in it.*

*And the Lord said unto Satan, Hast thou considered my servant Job, that there is none like him in the earth, a perfect and an upright man, one that feareth God, and escheweth evil?*

When I was three years old I was adopted. I never knew my birth father. I was adopted into a wonderful family. We all had our issues but I have been truly blessed to be in this family. One thing that I have always tried to do is make my father proud of me. I think that I have a misconception. I have thought that if I could only be better or do something else then I would make my Dad proud. I have continuously tried and tried to become better just to please him. I was thinking about this the other day and God made it very apparent that my goal should be to hear "Well done my good and faithful servant". He didn't say well done my perfect servant. He just said my good and faithful servant. God wants us to be faithful servants. Let us be like Job who was called God's servant. He was upright, without blame. He feared God and ran from evil. Job was a "good and faithful servant". May I become like him.

---

## NEWS OF THE DAY
### Tue 22-Feb-05

*BAGHDAD, Iraq -- A suicide bombing attack in Baghdad was prevented when police arrested a man before he could detonate his explosive belt. Police arrested a Sudanese man who was attempting to detonate his explosives inside of the Adnan Khairallah hospital.*

# Wed 23-Feb-05

Genesis 12:4, 5

*So Abram departed, as the Lord had spoken unto him; and Lot went with him; and Abram was seventy and five years old when he departed out of Haran.*

*And Abram took Sarai his wife, and Lot his brother's son, and all their substance that they had gotten in Haran; and they went forth to go into the land of Canaan; and into the land of Canaan they came.*

In the preceding verses God told Abram to leave the country that he knew, to leave his extended family and to go to a land that the Lord was going to show him. He then makes a covenant with Abram. The covenant was a promise to him that he would become a great nation. God would greatly bless Abram. He set aside Abram to be the father of the Hebrew nation, which in turn made him the Patriarch of the lineage of Christ. Abram didn't understand all of this when God told him to leave. All that he understood was that God told him to move and he obeyed. I think that it is interesting when he obeyed that he took his family with him. He didn't leave anyone behind for him to come back to. He didn't tell Sarai," Let me go and check this out and then I will come back to get you." He went out on blind faith. Hebrews 11:15 says, "And truly, if they had been mindful of that country from whence they came out, they might have had opportunity to have returned." This verse is discussing Abram and Sarai and the faith that they had. Abram did not leave anything to go back to. He truly trusted in Yahweh. He knew that God was Jehovah Jireh, God the Provider.

How is your faith? Is it strong enough to leave what you are doing and go to where God wants you to? Where is he telling you to go? What is He telling you to do? Listen to His still small voice and just GO!

# Thu 24-Feb-05

Ecclesiastes 7:9
*Be not hasty in they spirit to be angry: for anger resteth in the bosom of fools.*

As a somewhat natural redhead (when I have hair), I am the epitome of a hothead.  can be easily angered at little things. If things don't go my way then it will get under my skin and
really make me upset.        In this scripture the writer of Ecclesiastes says to not be hasty to become angry. There are times that it is okay to become angry. Even Jesus was angry when cleared out the temple. There were other times that he could have been easily angered though but he didn't. Some of those times were when James and John were arguing who would sit on Jesus right hand and who would sit on his left hand. Instead of getting angry he took the opportunity to teach them something. When He was praying in the Garden of Gethsemane, they fell asleep when they should have been watching and praying. Jesus woke them up twice to pray but they just couldn't stay awake. He could have easily gotten mad but instead he was gentle. We need to follow the example of Christ, and not be hasty to become angry.

# Fri 25-Feb-05

Philippians 4:11
*Not that I speak in respect of want: for I have learned, in whatsoever state I am, therewith to be content.*

Many children are not satisfied with what they have. I have a little girl who is going through stage. The other day my wife went shopping for some clothes for my daughter and my son. When my wife got home she got out the clothes and my daughter was excited to see the clothes. When my wife was done showing her the clothes my daughter said, "Is that ALL?" Isn't that the way we are with God? We always want more. Something I have learned while I have been here in Iraq is that I need to be content in everything. I have seen many people that are upset because they are not doing what they were trained to do. I have seen other people upset because they don't feel that they should have to do certain things. I have found a certain joy in just knowing that I am alive for another day. We must be content.

## Sun 27-Feb-05

Ephesians 5:25, 28
*Husbands, love your wives, even as Christ also loved the church, and gave himself for it;*
*So ought men to love their wives as their own bodies. He that loveth his wife loveth himself.*

Picture for a moment that Christ is here and taking care of us. He is there protecting us and providing for our needs. He looks at us with loving arms and wants us to know just how much he loves us. He loved us so much that he died for us. So it is in marriage. I love my wife so much that I would die for her. I have an awesome wife. She is continually letting me know just how much she truly loves me. We are best friends. When we talk on the phone she is always asking me, "Just five more minutes, please, five more minutes." She tells everyone about everything that is going on with me.

Now look at yourself and your relationship with Christ. Are you letting Christ know how much you love him? Do you ask for five more minutes when talking to him? Do you go around and tell other people about how proud you are of your Lord. (I am not calling myself my wife's lord). What type of relationship do you have with Him?

Thought for the day: Do you love your Lord and Savior as much or more than you love your wife or husband? How can you change that?

75

# Mon 28-Feb-05

Genesis 2:23-25
*And Adam said, This is now bone of my bones, and flesh of my flesh: she shall be called Woman, because she was taken out of Man.*
*Therefore shall a man leave his father and his mother, and shall cleave unto his wife: and they shall be one flesh.*
*And they were both naked, the man and his wife, and were not ashamed.*

What ever happened to the age of innocence? We live in a world when men and women have to plan who their date is going to be for that night. Sex is an everyday word. Children know more about intimacy more than adults do. This was not what God had intended. God's intention was that Adam would have a helpmate, a confidant, a friend, a lover. They would share everything with each-other. Man has taken God's plan and destroyed it. Instead of love you have lust. Instead of a friend they become enemies. Everyone is out for number one. Whatever makes me feel good. This is what has stolen our innocence. When is enough, enough? When will we stop handing condoms out in school and start telling children that God created sex for after marriage, between one man and one woman? We must take a stand! The age of innocence is in the past but we can still protect the innocence of our children. Take a stand today!

---

## NEWS OF THE DAY
Mon 28-Feb-05

*BAGHDAD, Iraq -- A suicide car bomber detonated his vehicle Monday in a crowd of people applying for jobs in Iraq's new security forces. At least 120 people died and 130 were wounded in the deadliest single attack of the nearly 2-year-old insurgency.*

# -FIELD NOTES-
*for Journaling*

# MARCH 2005

# Tue 01-Mar-05

Genesis 3:8-10

*And they heard the voice of the Lord God walking in the garden in the cool of the day: and Adam and his wife hid themselves from the presence of the Lord God amongst the trees of the garden.*

*And the Lord God called unto Adam, and said unto him, Where art thou?*

*And he said, I heard thy voice in the garden, and I was afraid, because I was naked; and I hid myself.*

Yesterday we talked about innocence. The question was what ever happened to man's innocence. In the verses prior to this man disobeyed God and ate of the tree of the knowledge of good and evil. That innocence was broken. Man realized how vulnerable he truly was. Verse 10 here has two meanings. The literal meaning was that they were without clothes. The second meaning, I believe, is that they realized they no longer had the protection that God had for them. They were spiritually unprotected. They were in the darkness. We are still in that darkness. The only way to come out of the darkness and be spiritually protected is through God's redemption.

In verse 15 of this chapter we have the first look at what God's plan for our redemption will be. We will discuss that in detail tomorrow.

# Wed 02-Mar-05

Romans 5:12-15

*Wherefore, as by one man sin entered into the world, and death by sin; and so death passed upon all men, for that all have sinned:*

*(For until the law sin was in the world: but sin is not imputed when there is no law.*

*Nevertheless death reigned from Adam to Moses, even over*

*them that had not sinned after the similitude of Adam's transgression,*
*who is the figure of him that was to come.*
    *But not as the offence, so also is the free gift. For if through the*
*offence of one many be dead, much more the grace of God, and the gift*
*by grace, which is by one man, Jesus Christ, hath abounded unto many.*

For the past couple of days I have talked about the age of
innocence. I discussed how innocence was taken away due to
man's sin. We will never have the innocence that we once had.
Sin entered the world. It will be there until the end of days. We
do have hope though. Just as sin entered into the world
through Adam, Christ has overcome that sin for all of us. We
have been justified in him. Verse 1 of Chapter 5 says that
because we are justified by our faith that we can have peace with
God through Jesus. We no longer have to hide from God. Jesus
has taken our place and replaced our guilt with innocence.
    When you go before God's throne, is He going to declare
your innocence or is he going to declare his verdict? How do
you know that you are innocent? Will He see your acceptance
of His Son's free gift? All it takes is a little bit of FAITH.

---

## NEWS OF THE DAY
### Wed 02-Mar-05

*BAGHDAD, Iraq -- A suicide car bomb detonated outside an Iraqi Army*
*recruiting center at the Al-Muthanna Airport Army Base in Baghdad, killing*
*six people and wounding twenty-eight others, including many civilians. The*
*bomb was detonated in a crowd of people waiting to submit recruitment papers*
*for the Iraqi Army. The group affiliated with Abu Musab al-Zarqawi,*
*Tanzim Qa'idat Al-Jihad fi Bilad al-Rafidayn, claimed responsibility for the*
*blast.*

87

# Thur 03-Mar-05

Corinthians 1:27
*But God hath chosen the foolish things of the world to*
*confound the wise; and God hath chosen the weak things of the*
*world to confound the things which are mighty;*

I have been taking a class on the Book of Genesis. In that
class we have discussed the different views of creation. It is
amazing how man has to try to understand everything. We have
to try to date everything and understand how the world came into
existence. It is in·our nature to be inquisitive but sometimes we
take things to the extreme. This verse in 1 Corinthians is really
true. If you look in the verses prior to this it talks about how the
Jews require a sign to believe and the Greeks sought after wisdom.
Many of us today require a sign from God to know that he is
there. Other people are looking for any other way to understand
how the earth came into being so that they can discredit God.
There are many "scientific" theories as to how the earth came into
being. Some of those theories are ludicrous, but many of those
theories have made people more confused than ever. Sometimes it
is just easier to let what God said in the scriptures be Gospel and
not try to change things to try to discredit Him.

---

## NEWS OF THE DAY
Thu 03-Mar-05

*BAQUBAH, Iraq -- A suicide bomber detonated his vehicle outside the*
*headquarters for the Iraqi emergency police in Baqubah, killing one person*
*and wounding at least eighteen others, including five policemen. Officials*
*believe the target of the attack was Mudhafar Shahab Jiburi, chief of the police*
*agency in Diyala province, whose convoy was nearby at the time. The group*
*affiliated with Abu Musab al-Zarqawi,Tanzim Qaidat Al-Jihad fi Bilad*
*al-Rafidayn, claimed responsibility for the attack.*

# Fri 04-Mar-05

*Read Psalms 46*

Psalms 46:10
*Be still, and know that I am God: I will be exalted among the heathen, I will be exalted in the earth.*

This morning when I sat down for my quiet time something came over me. I almost felt like God was telling me to be still. When I write these devotionals I try to set a time aside daily so that I can read and understand what God is telling me for that day's word. I try to do it first thing in the morning because if I don't then there are other distractions that will cause me to lose

focus. When I get here to do the word I sometimes get preoccupied with taking care of the message rather than listening to what God wants me to learn from the message. When I sat down this morning I asked God to let me know where to go today and at that moment is when I felt him say, "Be still".

When you read this whole chapter, there is turmoil going on. There are earthquakes, floods, landslides, and wars. Doesn't this sound like what has been happening recently? Amidst all of this going on, God tells us to be still. It is when we are still that His power and will is felt.

God has a plan for you wherever you are. The question is have you taken time to be still long enough to find out what that plan is?

# Sun 06-Mar-05

Thessalonians 2:2-3
*That ye be not soon shaken in mind, or be troubled, neither by spirit, nor by word, nor by letter as from us, as that the day of Christ is at hand.*

*Let no man deceive you by any means: for that day shall not come, except there come a falling away first, and that man of sin be revealed, the son of perdition;*

Every day as I read the newspaper, I see where there are people that want to discredit the Word of God. They want to take the Ten Commandments out of the court system. They want to take God out of everything. We are becoming a shaken people. We are being deceived in many ways. Satan wants for us to be so confused that we don't which way to turn. This verse is a two fold verse. Not only is it telling us to not let our minds be shaken. We know what God's word says. We need to be strong in our faith. Secondly this verse is giving us a sign. It is telling us that there will be people that are going to be deceived. They are going to fall away. Once that happens then Christ will come back. Be aware! Satan is !lurking about and he is waiting until just the right time and then he will try to attack your belief system. Will you be ready?

# Mon 07-Mar-05

Proverbs 16:1
*The preparations of the heart in man, and the answer of the tongue, is from the Lord.*

Recently my heart has been heavy. I have been stumbling around and am becoming more agitated with little things. I wonder sometimes where my joy has gone. When I read this verse I realize that God must prepare my heart. I must allow him the time to work. Sometimes you just keep going and never take time to be still and rest. If I allow God to prepare my heart and truly fill it then the answers that I give will be joyful again.

One thing that I have noticed about what God has been showing me here in Iraq over the past months is that I need to take time specifically for him and me to commune. The mentorship of an individual can't begin when there are many people around. God has a lot of things that he wants us to do but he must first prepare our hearts to be able to do his bidding. Sometimes we have such big plans for what we want God's plan to be that we never are actually doing what He wants us to. His true purpose is for us to serve Him wholeheartedly. That means we have to let him prepare it first. I was watching our workers the other day as they were putting concrete on the walls. The first thing they had to do was chip away the rough edges. Once they did that they could then put up the concrete. That is the way it is for us. God must chip away the junk that is in our heart to make room for what he has in store for you. He has some wonderful plans prepared for us. We must just be willing to allow him entrance into our heart so that he can prepare it.

NEWS OF THE DAY
Mon 07-Mar-05

*BAQUBAH, Iraq -- A suicide car bomb exploded outside an Iraqi police station, near a police convoy in Baqubah, killing eleven people and wounding at least twenty others. The dead included at least two police, three soldiers, and three civilians. This was one of several attacks in Baqubah on this day. This and the other Baqubah attacks were claimed by the group affiliated with Abu Musab al-Zarqawi,Tanzim Qa'idat Al-Jihad fi Bilad al-Rafidayn.*

## Tue 08-Mar-05

Ruth 1:16

*And Ruth said, Intreat me not to leave thee, or to return from following after thee: for whither thou goest, I will go; and where thou lodgest, I will lodge; thy people shall be my people, and thy God my God:*

Family is a big deal here in Iraq. I was hearing a story of a soldier that brought shoes and supplies for some of the Iraqi workers. The laborers were working in flip flops. The workers were all excited. The next day the workers showed up in flip flops again. When they were asked where the new shoes were they said that they gave them to their family members. There are many times that we in American society want to do away with family. No longer do we take care of our loved ones. Instead we put them in a nursing home to be cared for by a stranger because we just don't want to be bothered. We allow our family members to starve even though we have the means to help them out. In the scripture for today we read that Ruth (who was a daughter in law) wanted to go with Naomi. It didn't matter where she went, Ruth was going with her. When she married Naomi's son she was dedicating herself to his family for life. What a powerful way to look at our society. Every culture is different but I think that as Americans if we could take something from the Iraqis it would be the fact that they are dedicated to their family no matter what.

---

NEWS OF THE DAY
Tue 08-Mar-05

*BAGHDAD, Iraq -- Two women wearing suicide bombing explosive belts and were planning to blow up the al-Iskandariyah court building were arrested before they could carry out their attack. Four potential suicide bombers were arrested in the city on this day. All four women confessed to working with the Islamic Army in Iraq.*

# Wed 09-Mar-05

*Read Numbers 2*

Numbers 2:34
*And the children of Israel did according to all that the Lord commanded Moses: so they pitched by their standards, and so they set forward, every one after their families, according to the house of their fathers.*

When I arrived in to Camp Virginia, Kuwait all I saw was a dust bowl with a bunch of tents arranged neatly in rows. There were different areas set aside for different units. Our Battalion lived in Pad 8. As I looked around I started seeing different unit guidons or flags being flown to signify what unit was staying there. It made life so much easier. When we had to find a soldier from A Company all we had to do was look for the A Company guidon. We knew that the company operations would be able to tell us where that soldier was.

In the text for today we read that the Israelites were divided up by family name. They were then sent out to certain areas to live and protect the camp. The way that they knew what family was where was by the Standard or Flag that was flown. Take for example the tribe of Judah. Judah had 74,600 men. It was their job to secure the east side of the camp along with the tribes of Issachar and Zebulun. The only way that the men knew where to go was by looking for their Standard that was flying. When that Standard moved then they moved. When the Standard stopped then they stopped and made camp;

In life we must rally around something as well. If not we will become lost. Most Christians have a church home that is where their Standard is flown. The Nation of Israel had twelve tribes in it. They were all there for the same cause but they were all maybe a little bit different. In the Christian church family there are different denominations. Most of these denominations have the same overall belief system. They all rally around the Cross but each might have a different Standard that they might fly. Some might fly the Baptist Standard, others might fly the Methodist. Some might fly the Catholic Standard. The real question that must be asked though is whether the Standard that they are flying, matches up to the TRUE STANDARD of the Bible. If it does then they are all fighting the same battle just under different Flags. If the Standard that they are fighting under doesn't match up with the Bible then it would be wise and necessary to move to a church that does align itself with the Bible. We must ensure that we are all fighting for the same cause and that is the Cause of Christ.

---

## NEWS OF THE DAY
Wed 09-Mar-05

*BAGHDAD, Iraq -- Two suicide bombers blew up a large garbage truck in front of the Al-Sadir Hotel used by foreigners and contractors and the Agriculture Ministry building. The Ministry building was set on fire by the explosion and about twenty cars were severely damaged. The bombers were able to gain access to the compound housing the two buildings after a group of gunmen wearing police uniforms shot two guards at the checkpoint. Guards shot at the vehicle to prevent a large explosion, but failed to prevent the suicide bombers. At least four people were killed and forty wounded in the attack, including thirty American contractors. The group affiliated with Abu Musab al-Zarqawi, Tanzim Qa'idat Al-Jihad fi Bilad al-Rafidayn, claimed responsibility for the attack. On March 21, the US military reported that it had captured ten men who admitted planning and carrying out the attack.*

# Thu 10-Mar-05

Matthew 13:3-9
*And he spake many things unto them in parables, saying, Behold, a sower went forth to sow And when he sowed, some seeds fell by the wayside, and the fowls came and devoured them up:*
*Some fell upon stony places, where they had not much earth: and forthwith they sprung up, because they had no deepness of earth:*
*And when the sun was up, they were scorched; and because they had no root, they withered away.*
*And some fell among thorns; and the thorns sprung up, and choked them:*
*But other fell into good ground, and brought forth fruit, some an hundredfold, some sixty fold, some thirtyfold.*
*Who hath ears to hear, let him hear.*

I have been putting in a garden around my work area here. Since I am here in Mesopotamia and the Fertile Crescent I thought it might be a good idea to see just how fertile it really is. I have dug the dirt by hand and turned it over. I built my rows and then I sowed the seeds. I put 3 or 4 seeds per hole and then carefully covered them. I watered them. As I was planting these seeds my interpreter was helping me. It was the perfect opportunity to discuss this verse. She has been reading her Bible and asking me questions as she comes to some thing that she doesn't understand. We discussed how some of the seeds will not take root. Other seeds will grow fast but will not be strong. Then there will be still others that will have weeds that will come and choke them out. The final ones will grow to fruition and will produce fruit.

We then discussed what this meant for the Word. Many times we present the Word.

People will listen to it and it will perk their interest. But then work and their busy life will block out the word and it will die.

For others the word will be planted in a life that is on the rocks. The person that has that type of life is just trying to "get through". When the word comes there the roots never take hold and the word dies. For others there are many things that pop up in their life that causes them to lose faith. Their faith dies because everything else has blocked out the SON. Then there are the people that hear the word and accept it and grow.

As I look at these people I see us as Christians that we have a large responsibility to help all of these people. First of all when you plant a garden you don't plant it on rocky ground. You must work to soften the dirt. We must be willing to listen to others who have a problem.

Sometimes you can help to remove some of the rocks in people's lives. We can also help weed people's lives. The best way to do that is by praying for them. Sometimes we can help them get rid of some of the weeds depending on what they are. As a gardener you must take of your garden. As a person who is spreading God's seed you must be able to help tend the seed as well.

---

### NEWS OF THE DAY
### Thu 10-Mar-05

*MOSUL, Iraq -- A suicide bomber blew himself up Thursday during a funeral at a Shiite mosque in this northern city, killing 47 people and injuring more than 100, witnesses and local hospital officials said. They said the 5:30 p.m. blast occurred at the al-Shahidain al-Sadir Mosque when a man detonated an explosives belt he was wearing in a tent next to the mosque where mourners were gathering for dinner. Television footage showed white plastic chairs overturned and personal effects scattered on a dirt floor covered with blood.*

## Fri 11-Mar-05

Psalms 84:10
*For a day in thy courts is better than a thousand, I had rather be a doorkeeper in the house of my God, than to dwell in the tents of wickedness.*

There is a song that I have heard recently that says "Better is one day in your Courts than A thousand elsewhere". Our desire should be to want to be in God's presence. When we are out of His presence then we are dwelling in the tents of wickedness. I can imagine being a doorkeeper in the house of God. I would be continually opening the door for other people to enter. As I opened the door I am able to see what is outside those heavenly realms. I imagine that I could see many dark and dangerous things. I am glad that God has prepared a place for me so that I can at least be a servant in heaven rather than the alternative elsewhere. God's plan is that we all want to be in his courts communing with Him. That is what we were created for. We were created to have fellowship with him. There are many of us who would rather live in the tent of wickedness, because we want to have "fun". Well that fun is short lived. Soon it becomes very painful and you are wishing that you were back in the courts of God again. Choose today to leave the tents of wickedness and move into the courts of God. It is a whole lot more fun there.

## Sat 12-Mar-05

Numbers 4:1
*And the Lord spake unto Moses and unto Aaron, saying,*

To some people, the book of Numbers can be a very dry book. It seems that it is all about how people were numbered and told to go places and do certain things. What really impresses me is the fact that Numbers shows God playing an active role in the lives of the Children of Israel. In chapter 4 alone "and the Lord spake", is quoted three times. In the first four chapters it is quoted ten times. God's plan was unique and required his complete involvement.

How much involvement does God have in your life? What has he said unto you recently? Were you listening? Try to listen to God's voice; he has a specific plan for your life.

# Sun 13-Mar-05

*Read Daniel 6*

Daniel 6:16
*Then the king commanded, and they brought Daniel, and cast him into the dens of lions. Now the king spake and said unto Daniel, Thy God whom thou servest continually, he will deliver thee.*

Daniel was being thrown to the lions for praying to God. King Darius had been tricked into trapping Daniel. The other princes of the region didn't like Daniel. He was the king's right hand man. Everyone else was jealous of him. They devised a way for Daniel to be done away with. You see Daniel was predictable. He could always be seen praying to God three times a day. The other rulers knew that he would continue to do it. The question before us today though is why was Daniel so predictable? Daniel was in love with his creator. He had been through a lot with God. God had taken him through the turmoil of working for Nebuchadnezzar. He had predicted the fall of Babylon and it happened. Through all of the wickedness of the known world Daniel had remained true to God. Now Darius was in a bad predicament. He had signed a written decree that said that if you were caught praying to anybody except to the king that you would be thrown into the lion's den. If he went back on his decree then he was a weak man. If he threw Daniel into the lions then he lost one of his best wise men. Darius knew that Daniel's faith would carry him through because of Daniel's life that had been lived before. That is why Darius said, "Thy God whom thou servest continually, he will deliver thee."

When your life comes under scrutiny do people look at you and say "there is a man or woman of God"? Do they look at you differently than they would look at their other friends? Are you living a life like Daniel, that when he was brought to the test others knew that his God was going to take care of him?

Thought for the day: Can others see my Lord through me?

97

# Mon 14-Mar-05

1 John 1:8-10
*If we say that we have no sin, we deceive ourselves, and the truth is not in us.*

*If we confess our sins, he is faithful and just to forgive us our sins, and to cleanse us from all unrighteousness.*

*If we say that we have not sinned, we make him a liar, and his word is not in us:*

Man is inherently evil. Every man has sinned except Jesus Christ. It is in our blood line to sin. I am currently taking a class on the book of Genesis. The instructor was discussing sin and the consequences of sin. The question was raised as to why bad things happen to people. For many people there is the assumption that the individual sinned and therefore he is being punished for his sin by contracting this horrible illness, for example. Sin is the cause of the illness but it may not have been that person's sin. God's punishment for sin is death. Because of the consequence of sin then many people become ill.

In English class I always enjoyed the "if... then" statements. Verse 9 is a perfect if then statement. If we confess our sins... then he will forgive our sins and cleanse us from all unrighteousness. The amazing thing is that God is faithful. We don't find many people that are faithful to their promises but God is faithful to HIS. The true question is will we be faithful and humble enough to confess our sins. Humility is the key.

Lord, give me the courage to be able to confess my sins and the humility to accept your forgiveness. AMEN

---

NEWS OF THE DAY
Mon 14-Mar-05

*BAGHDAD, Iraq -- A suicide bomber detonated his vehicle as he approached a police and army checkpoint north of Baghdad, The attack killed two policemen and two civilians. No group claimed responsibility for the attack.*

# Tue 15-Mar-05

Malachi 1: 6-8

*A son honoureth his father, and a servant his master: if then I be a father, where is mine honour? And if I be a master, where is my fear? Saith the Lord of hosts unto you, O priests, that despise my name. And say, wherein have we despised thy name?*

*Ye offer polluted bread upon mine altar; and ye say, wherein have we polluted thee? In that ye say, the table of the Lord is contemptible.*

*And if ye offer the blind for sacrifice, is it not evil? And if ye offer the lame and sick, is it not evil? Offer it now unto thy governor; will he be pleased with thee, or accept thy person? Saith the lord of hosts.*

God was extremely upset with the Israelites. He was even more upset with the priests. Here the people were trying to get with doing the bare minimum for him. God wanted their best for an offering. Instead they were giving their blind, lame sheep as a sacrifice. They were just going through the rituals. Their desire to serve God had grown old. Instead they were just going through the motions. Who cares what they were giving Him. It was still a sacrifice. God wanted their best.

Now look at your life. How is your life like the Israelites? Have you lost your fire for Him? I was encouraged to read the book of Malachi last night. The book is filled with a lot of inspirational guidance for life. God doesn't want us to be going through the motions. He wants our whole hearts. How many times do we give God just enough of our time to "get by"? I know that it is so hard in the morning to get up and do PT let alone anything else. God wants to be our life not just a piece of it.

Thought For the day: How can I give more to God today than I have ever given before?

*BAGHDAD, Iraq -- A suicide bomber detonated his vehicle in northeast Baghdad near a police patrol. The bomber missed the police patrol and crashed into a tree, killing a child and wounding four other people.*

# Wed 16-Mar-05

*Read Numbers 10:1-10*

*And if ye go to war in your land against the enemy that oppresseth you, then ye shall blow an alarm with trumpets; and ye shall be remembered before the Lord your God, and ye shall be saved from your enemies.*

In the military we have different signals that mean different things. One long blast on a horn means... Three short blasts means... Metal banging against metal in a certain pattern means... If you are not a soldier in the US Army then you don't ·know what I am talking about. If you are then you know exactly what each means. During World War II there were sirens that were used to announce air-raids. Today in the Plains states where tornadoes are prevalent there are towers that have horns on them to announce when a tornado is coming.

In our reading today, God has instructed the people of Israel how to communicate with each other. Remember there were literally hundreds of thousands of people who made up the nation of Israel. There was no way to communicate with each tribe. Noise was the best way to communicate different messages. God is giving us a visual representation of what will happen when Christ comes back. 1 Thessalonians 4:16, details how we will be called home. It says this, "For the Lord himself shall descend from heaven with a shout, with the voice of the archangel, and then with the trump of God: and the dead in Christ shall rise first." God will use the trumpet to announce Christ's return and the rapture of the Church. Only those who know the Lord will understand the trumpet sound. Only they will be called home. All others will be left to go through the great Tribulation.

Where will you be? Will you hear the trumpet and understand, or will you be confused?

Search your heart and if you don't know then I would beg you to ask Christ to forgive you for your sins and accept his gift of salvation. That is the only way that you will know the trumpet sound.

## Thur 17-Mar-05

Psalm 77:1
*I cried unto God with my voice, even unto God with my voice; and he gave ear unto me.*

About three months ago, there was a soldier who was constantly late for formation. I was in charge of the local national workers escort detail. At the time we had formations 3 times a day. We had one at 0500, for initial accountability. The next formation was at 0550 to ensure that all personnel showed back for duty. The last formation was at 1730 so that we could find out who was on the detail for the next day. This soldier was late on a regular basis. As a form of corrective training, I instructed him to write an essay on the importance of punctuality. In that essay he explained how the people prior to me had only had one formation and that he wasn't used to so many formations. Through the essay I began to be understanding of the fact that there were too many formations. I rescinded the policy of so many formations.

In the verse today the author is talking about how he cried unto God. He cried and God heard his cry. There are many times that we think that our issues are not big enough for God to hear. We think that He won't have time for our little issues. We must be able to communicate our needs to him. In Genesis the Bible talks about how God created us to communicate with us.

When man sinned the communication chain was broken. God still wants to communicate with us. Let us cry unto him and share our hearts with Him. He will give ear to our cry.

# Fri 18-Mar-05

1 Corinthians 4:1-2

*Let a man so account of us, as of the ministers of Christ, and stewards of the mysteries of God.*

*Moreover it is required in stewards, that a man be found faithful.*

Someone is always watching you. When I was a kid I used to do a lot of stupid things. I would try to do things that I wasn't supposed to do. I always thought that I would be able to get away with it. Then I would go home and my parents would ask me about it. I never could understand how my parents would find out what I had done. They would just smile and say, "Someone is always watching you." Now that I am a parent I know exactly what they mean. I have people all the time telling me what my children have done. It doesn't matter if it has been good or bad; someone is always telling me about them.

As a believer, we always have people watching us. People don't care what you say.

They care about what you do. They watch us to see what we will do in certain situations. Sometimes they may just do something to see you react. How you react will play a lot in how they perceive Christians. One of the biggest reasons that people don't go to church is because there are a "bunch of hypocrites there." People want to see you say one thing and do something else. We must be found faithful. As God's word says, men will hold us accountable for the actions that we do. If we are God's children then we must remain faithful to Him and his Word.

Lord, Let my life be seen as faithful to you. May my words and my life match up and be seen as being used as a vessel for you. Amen.

# Sat 19-Mar-05

Matthew 6:25-26

*Therefore I say unto you, Take no thought for your life, what ye shall eat, or what ye shall drink; nor yet for your body, what ye shall put on. Is not the life more than meat, and the body more than raiment?*

*Behold the fowls of the air: for they sow not, neither do they reap, nor gather into barns; yet your heavenly Father feedeth them. Are ye not much better than they?*

Every morning when I walk to work I am reminded of this verse. There are little birds that are flying everywhere. They are eating and drinking water and they are singing. It is the most beautiful sound when you walk out of your trailer and hear birds singing. It truly makes me stop and realize just how blessed I really am. When I am back in the States everything is hustle and bustle. We have to get to PT by 0545 and to work call by 0900. I sit in an office pretty much all day. I very rarely get the opportunity to stop and look at what God has created. When I get up here, I can take a little time to slow down and smell the roses. It is almost as if God is giving me an opportunity to look at the world from a different perspective.

When you have all the worries of the world coming down on you there is always the tendency to worry and fret the small stuff. This verse is just for those who worry. If God will take care of the sparrows or birds then I know He will take care of your problems too.

We just need to trust Him with our issues.

# Sun 20-Mar-05

*Read Mark 11:1-11*

Mark 11:8-9
*And they brought the colt to Jesus, and cast their garments on him; and he sat upon him.*
*And many spread their garments in the way: and others cut down branches off the trees, and strawed them in the way.*
*And they that went before, and they that followed, cried, saying, Hosanna; Blessed is he that cometh in the name of the Lord:*

Here is Jesus coming into Jerusalem knowing that he is to die here one week later. What is interesting here is that Jesus is actually entering the city as a willing participant. He is not being forced to enter. He is riding on a lowly colt. This colt has never been ridden before. In fact according to Matthew the disciples had to get not only the colt but also the donkey. This was probably because the colt wouldn't have even left the mother. Nowhere in scripture though does it say that Jesus was thrown off the colt. There were crowds everywhere and the noise level had to be tremendous but the colt just walked along. I think this is because it was Christ on his back. Jesus tends to have a calming effect on many things. Jesus calmed the storm. He calmed a crowd that wanted to stone someone the prostitute. He can calm your heart if you let him. In life things get so busy that it seems like we are going to get thrown off the horse that we are riding.

We must ask Jesus to calm our hearts and see what really matters. Then and only then can we move forward into battle.

NEWS OF THE DAY
Sun 20-Mar-05

*FALLUJA, Iraq -- A suicide bomber detonated his vehicle near a convoy of foreigners. The attack occurred in Fallujah. Two Iraqi civilians were killed in the attack.*

# Mon 21-Mar-05

Malachi 2:12-14
*The Lord will cut off the man that doeth this, the master of the scholar, out of the tabernacles of Jacob, and him that offereth an offering unto the Lord of hosts.*

*And this have ye done again, covering the altar of the Lord with tears, with weeping, and with crying out, insomuch that he regardeth not the offering any more, or receiveth it with good will at your hand.*

*Yet ye say, Wherefore? Because the Lord hath been witness between thee and the wife of thy youth, against whom thou hast dealt treacherously: yet is she thy companion, and the wife of thy covenant.*

Divorce is rampant in the world. When I was growing up I remember hearing statistics that said 1 in 4 people were divorcing. I thought that was bad, but now 4 marriages out of every 1000 ends in divorce. When a man and woman get they married they become one flesh. They make a covenant with each other and with God that they will be married forever. There is supposed to be a commitment but in today's society there seems to be a big problem with commitment.

Commitment is the overlying problem. No longer do people consider their word their bond. Instead there is this feeling of carelessness. "I really just don't like this person any more, so I will just divorce them." As marriage is being diluted by divorce so goes the morals and values of our country. We must look into our hearts and find that commitment that we have lost. God's will is that we marry one spouse. He wants to help create the bond that can't be broken.

*SAMARRA, Iraq -- A suicide bomber detonated a truck filled with explosives near a hospital in Samarra. Several homes were damaged and about 12 people were wounded. The attack would have caused more damage, but the driver detonated the explosives too early.*

# Wed 23-Mar-05

*Read Psalm 99*

Psalm 99:9
*Exalt the LORD our God, and worship at his holy hill; for the LORD our God is holy.*

Have you ever just sat down and thanked God for who He is? I think that it is so hard to praise God for all of His magnitude because I can't fathom it all. It is hard enough for me to praise someone that I know for something that they did. I remember as a child that I enjoyed being praised for the job that I have done. I had a soldier the other day ask me if he was doing a good job. He was looking for someone to take notice in him. He was hoping someone would think that he was doing a good job. I often wonder how God feels. The Psalmist writes that we should exalt the Lord. We should praise Him because he is Holy. He is a just God. God wants to have us come and tell him how glad we are that he is a holy, blameless God. He just wants to hear from us. I think that this one of the hardest things for believers to do. We are quick to tell God what we need or what someone else needs, but how slow we are to praise him for who He is and what He has created. Let us strive today to truly praise God for who He is.

# Thu 24-Mar-05

Haggai 1:3-7

*Then came the word of the LORD by Haggai the prophet, saying,*

*Is it time for you, O ye, to dwell in you cieled houses, and this house lie waste?*

*Now therefore thus saith the LORD of hosts; Consider your ways.*

*Ye have sown much, and bring in little; ye drink, but ye have not enough; ye drink, but ye are not filled with drink; ye clothe you, but there is none warm; and he that earneth wages earneth wages to put it into a bag with holes.*

*Thus saith the LORD of hosts; Consider your ways.*

The Temple in Jerusalem had been destroyed by the Babylonians. As the Israelites had slowly made their way back to Jerusalem they rebuilt the wall around the city, and they rebuilt their houses. They had not rebuilt the Temple. These people were more concerned about their well being than they were about their relationship with God. In this verse the Lord is asking when they will think of Him. When will they rebuild His house? I think it is important that the test reading has in it twice, "Consider your ways". God is asking for his children to think about what they are doing and why they are doing it. He then proceeds to ask them some questions about why they seem to be living poorly. He says, "Why do you think that everything you make seems to disappear?" Everyone seemed to be holding out on God.

What are you holding out on God with today? Does He want some of your time and you won't give it to Him? Does He want to be Lord of your life and you still want to be in control? In the scripture today it shows that you won't find fulfillment until you give Him all of what He is asking for. He wants you!

*RAMADI, Iraq -- A suicide bomber detonated his vehicle at a checkpoint in Ramadi, killing eleven Iraqi special police commandos and wounding at least fourteen other people, including nine police officers and three civilians. The Islamic Army in Iraq posted a statement on the internet claiming responsibility for this attack.*

# Fri 25-Mar-05

John 19:26-27

*When Jesus therefore saw his mother, and the disciple standing by, whom he loved, he saith unto his mother, Woman, behold thy son!*

*Then saith he to the disciple, Behold thy mother! And from that hour that disciple took her unto his own home.*

Jesus is now on the cross. He has been beaten. He has the crown of thorns on his head. He has had to stumble down the road as he carried his own cross. He has had people yell at him and curse him. Then the Roman soldiers hammered spikes through his hands and his feet. They put him up for everyone to see and he was dying as the criminals to the left and right would. But Jesus had some unfinished business. He saw his mother and he thought of her.

Jesus was still filled with compassion even when he was in tremendous pain and on the verge of death.

Jesus was also thinking of us as he was on that cross. He knew that the only way that man would ever have fellowship with the Father again was if he paid the ultimate price for sin. He had to stay on that cross for you and me. So, not only was he thinking of his mother and making provisions for her, He was also thinking of you and me as he was making ultimate provision for you with his heavenly father. This is just an awesome thought that Christ would want to spend eternity with you and me.

# Sat 26-Mar-05

Matthew 28:18-20
*And Jesus came and spake unto them, saying, All power is given unto me in heaven and in earth.*
*Go ye therefore, and teach all nations, baptizing them in the name of the Father, and of the*
*Son, and of the Holy Ghost:*
*Teaching them to observe all things whatsoever I have commanded you" and, lo, I am with you always, even unto the end of the world. AMEN.*

My parents and I had a conversation before I went to Afghanistan, and then before I came over to Iraq. The conversation was in regards to sending forth their children as missionaries to foreign lands. As we were discussing I thought that it was ironic that I am not having to raise support, find my own lodging, or do anything that most missionaries have to do prior to leaving for the mission field. Instead, I just get the opportunity to go to the ends of the earth for the United States of America but they are actually paying my bill as I work on fulfilling the Great Commission. I think that the purpose of the Great Commission was not only for the 11 disciples to go tell world about Jesus but it was also for all believers to continue to tell others about their wonderful Savior.

You don't have to go to Iraq or Afghanistan to tell others about Him. You can tell people about him in your own backyard. All you have to do is get the courage to tell someone. Once you do that God will give you the words to say. To borrow an old NIKE phrase: JUST DO IT!

# Sun 27-Mar-05

John 20:26-29
*And after eight days again his disciples were within, and Thomas with them: then came Jesus, the doors being shut, and stood in the midst, and said, Peace be unto you.*

*Then saith he to Thomas, Reach hither thy finger, and behold my hands; and reach hither thy hand, and thrust it into my side: and be not faithless, but believing.*

*And Thomas answered and said unto him, My Lord and my God.*

*Jesus saith unto him, Thomas, because thou hast seen me, thou hast believed: blessed are they that have not seen, and yet have believed.*

So here is Thomas, one of the Lord's chosen 12, who doesn't believe that Christ arose from the dead. He told the other disciples that unless he could actually see Jesus and put his hand in his side that he would not believe. Then Jesus comes in the room. That must have been a somewhat scary time. All of a sudden Jesus enters the room and comes directly over to Thomas. In essence Jesus tells Thomas I want you to believe so here I am. Thomas was in awe. I don't think that he actually even put his hand in Jesus side, or his finger in his hand. I think that as soon as Jesus said those words that Thomas believed.

What will it take for you to believe today that Christ is alive? If you do believe that He is alive, are you walking with joy in your heart? We should be excited that Jesus rose from the dead to overcome sin and death. We are no longer tied down by sin and we have everlasting life if we believe. Our souls will be with him forever. Alleluia.

## Mon 28-Mar-05

*Read Numbers 11*

Numbers 11:31-33

*And there went forth a wind from the Lord, and brought quails from the sea, and let them fall by the camp, as It were a day's journey on this side, and as it were day's journey on the other side, round about the camp, and as it were two cubits high upon the face of the earth.*

*And the people stood up all that day, and all that night and all the next day, and they gathered the quails: he that gathered least*

*gathered ten homers: and they spread them all abroad for themselves*
*round about the camp.*

*And while the flesh was yet between their teeth, ere it was*
*chewed the wrath of the Lord was kindled against the people, and the*
*Lord smote the people with a very great plague.*

While I have been stationed in Iraq I have noticed how
ungrateful some people are. We live in trailers, eat good food in the
Dining Facility, and take hot showers. We very rarely have to deal
with the enemy trying to attack us here. Recently though I have
noticed a trend. People are starting to complain about the food. They
are complaining about the trailers. They are complaining about not
getting a hot shower. It is if they think that they deserve all of this.
We are fighting a war and people think that we should have the same
things that we have back home.

There are many times in our life that we are ungrateful for
the simple things that are given to us. In the verses that we read
today we see that Israel was ungrateful for the food that God had
provided. Sometimes we get so hung up on ourselves and what we
want that we forget to be grateful for what God has blessed us with.
As you go about your day today be thankful for what God has given
you.

## Tue 29-Mar-05

Jude 1:17-22
*But, beloved, remember ye the words which were spoken before*
*of the apostles of our Lord Jesus Christ;*

*How that they told you there should be mockers in the last*
*time, who should walk after their own ungodly lusts.*

*These be they who separate themselves, sensual, having not the*
*Spirit.*

*But ye, beloved, building up yourselves on your most holy*
*faith, praying in the Holy Ghost,*

*Keeping yourselves in the love of God, looking for the mercy of*
*our Lord Jesus Christ unto eternal life.*

*And some have compassion, making a difference:*

Recently there have been a number of events in our world that have shown me that the Day of Our Lord is near. We have seen many earthquakes and natural disasters. We have seen nation rising against other nations. We are seeing life being starved out of a lady because she is not mentally all there. We see little girls abducted daily so that men can take advantage of them and then kill them. I can't believe what I am seeing. It pains my heart to see so many things going on and not know what I can do to stop it. I am a man of action. If I see a problem I try to face it head on and fix it. These are problems that I can't fix.

In the scripture reading today Jude is telling us to stay strong in our faith. We need to must stand on our faith. People around us are going to try to bring us down but we must let our faith in Jesus keep us strong. Then we must make a difference where we can. It is only through the saving love of Jesus that we can make a difference. We must be able to stand so that others can see our heavenly Father through us. Take heart God is in control and He needs you to stand with Him for Eternity.

# Sun 30-Mar-05

Micah 4:1-2

*But in the last days it shall come to pass, that the mountain of the house of the LORD shall be established in the top of the mountains, and it shall be exalted above the hills; and people shall flow unto it.*

*And many nations shall come, and say, Come, and let us go up to the mountain of the LORD, and to the house of the God of Jacob; and he will teach us of his ways, and we will walk in his paths: for the law shall go forth of Zion, and the word of the Lord from Jerusalem.*

A portion of Micah chapter 4 is a foretelling of the eternal kingdom. Nations will come together so that the Lord can teach us His ways. Then they will walk in the paths of Lord.

What amazes me is the fact that it seems to me that many people are waiting for that

day. They want to live their life for themselves and do whatever makes them feel good. We have people that are trying work their way to heaven. I am truly amazed at how the local people take their faith so seriously. Every day at certain times they go to prayer. They make sure that their hands and face are clean. Everything step is very important to them. I then look at people who call themselves Christians and see that they are no different than non-Christians. There is no evidence of their relationship with Christ. We as Christians should be living a life that lets the light of Christ shine so that others may flow to it and learn God's ways.

How long will we wait for the Lord to come back before we let His light shine through us.

He has given us the Holy Spirit to shine through us, so let Him SHINE!

## Thu 31-Mar-05

Genesis 6:8-9
*But Noah found grace in the eyes of the LORD.*
*These are the generations of Noah: Noah was a just man and perfect in his generations, and Noah walked with God.*

What are your goals in life? In the military we ask our soldiers what their short term goals are and what their long term goals are. We do this to ensure that the soldier is not just living in the now but that they are planning for their future. I remember when I was young I was extremely competitive. I always had to win. I had dreams of being the best. My goal was to be the best then. I wasn't thinking about the future.

In the scripture reading today we find a man who found grace in the eyes of the Lord. He also was a man that was perfect in his generation. In other words he was a righteous man. The climax of all of this was that Noah walked with God. Now what were Noah's goals? What type of life did he live? Was he out for himself or was he seeking God in everything that he did? The Bible doesn't say what prompted Noah to be righteous but it does say that God chose him because of his faith. In Hebrews 11:7 it says this, " By faith Noah,... became heir of the righteousness which is by faith." Noah's decision making was focused on one thing, his faith.

Because of his faith the Bible said that he walked with God.

As you look at your goals ask yourself if they line up with is God's will for your life. Let your life goal be that others see that you walked with God.

NEWS OF THE DAY
Thu 31-Mar-05

*HILLA, Iraq -- A suicide car bomb was detonated near a crowd of Shiite pilgrims on the road between Hilla and Karbala. The pilgrims were celebrating a major Shiite religious holiday by walking to Karbala. Seven people were killed and nice wounded in the attack.*

# -FIELD NOTES-
*for Journaling*

# APRIL & MAY 2005

# Fri 01-Apr-05

Genesis 2:7
*And the LORD God formed man of the dust of the
ground, and breathed into his nostrils the breath of life; and man
became a living soul.*

Over the past couple of weeks I have been watching the
Schiavo case unfold. I have seen anger and bitterness from both
sides and I have been concerned as it has played out just how this
would affect the case for the sanctity of life. For those of you who
haven't followed the news, Mary Schiavo was a lady that died
yesterday from her feeding tube being removed. She had been in a
vegetative state since 1990 and the courts decided that she
wouldn't want to live that type of life. There has been a lot of
arguments on whether she should live or not. As I was watching
this unfold I was reminded of this verse. God is the one that gives
life. We are not to take it away. If we do it is called murder. If we
look in Genesis 9:6 God is telling Noah what punishment will be
given for those who take someone's life. It says this, "Whoso
sheddeth man's blood by man shall his blood be shed: for in the
image of God made he man."

I am not just upset about the Schiavo case; I am seeing a
trend that is appearing. We as humans do not respect the sanctity
of life. We think that we are God and that we can decide when a
person should live or die. We must wake up and realize that God
will punish us. We are treading on very thin ice and He will have
the final say so. Life is precious. We must protect it at all cost.
From a soldier's perspective, it is my job to protect the lives of my
fellow soldiers as well as those of the innocent. It is also my job to
protect the inherent freedoms that our forefathers established.
Those freedoms are of LIFE, LIBERTY, and the PURSUIT OF
HAPPINESS. I can't protect those freedoms when they are taken
away from within. We must reevaluate our beliefs. We must
choose today whether we are going to serve our one and only
God, Yahweh, or are we going to play god and decide our destiny.

Joshua 24:15 says this, "And if it seem evil unto you to serve the LORD, choose you this day whom ye will serve; whether the gods which your fathers served that were on the other side of the flood, or the gods of the Amorites, in whose land ye dwell: but as for me and my house, we will serve the LORD. Make your choice today!

## Sat 02-Apr-05

2 Timothy 2:19-22
*Nevertheless the foundation of God standeth sure, having this seal, The Lord knoweth them that are his. And, Let everyone that nameth the name of Christ depart from iniquity.*
*But in a great house there are not only vessels of gold and silver, but also of wood and of*
*earth; and some to honour, and some to dishonour.*
*If a man therefore purge himself from these, he shall be a vessel unto honour, sanctified, and meet for the master's use, and prepared unto every good work.*
*Flee also youthful lusts: but follow righteousness, faith, charity, peace, with them that call on the Lord out of a pure heart.*

When I was young I always enjoyed building forts in the woods behind our house. We lived in a section of northern Atlanta but we actually had woods between our house and the neighborhood behind us. I would take wood that I could find and we would build anything and everything. My parents specifically told me that I could build a roof but I could not get on top of it, but one time I thought I would build a treehouse. I had everything in place and climbed up on top when the wood that I had placed the flooring on shifted and I fell through. Luckily I wasn't hurt to bad but I learned my lesson.

Foundations are the key to a good building. Foundations are also the key in life. Our foundations must be placed on Christ. He is our cornerstone. As we build our walk with Christ we must flee the lusts that we had when we were not saved. We must pursue righteousness.

The picture that comes to mind is one of running away from a gang who want you to do something bad. We must run after righteousness. It won't wait for us. We won't be righteous where we stand; we must pursue it. Seek Christ's righteousness today to be your foundation in life.

---

*FALLUJAH, Iraq -- A Marine assigned to the 2nd Light Armored Reconnaissance Battalion, II Marine Expeditionary Force, was killed Saturday, April 2, by an explosion while conducting combat operations in Hadithah in support of Operation Iraqi Freedom.*

# Sun 03-Apr-05

Colossians 1:21-22
*And you, that were sometime alienated and enemies in your mind by wicked works, yet now hath he reconciled In the body of his flesh through death, to present you holy and unblameable and unreproveable in his sight:*

God wants us to be Holy and be reproach. This is the only way that He can commune with us. Man is inherently evil though, so God provided a way that we can be reconciled to Him. That way was through His Son's death. His shed blood was what made us holy. In God's eyes we are now pure.

It is if we are a clear glass. Inside there is water with black food coloring in it. It

represents sin. When Jesus cleans our heart it is like a dropper full of bleach being added to the water. The water becomes clear again. Once that happens we can see through to the other side. God wants to be able to look through our hearts and see no sin. That is why He sent Jesus to die for us. It is only through His blood that we can enter heaven. There is nothing that we can ever do that will allow us to be good enough to get to heaven. Let your prayer today be that Jesus will present you holy and blameless to the Father.

NEWS OF THE DAY
Sun 03-Apr-05

*BAGHDAD, Iraq -- Scores of insurgents mounted an audacious assault on Baghdad's Abu Ghraib jail over the weekend with a barrage of rockets, mortars, car bombs and small-arms fire that wounded at least 44 US troops and 12 prisoners. Between 40 and 60 attackers struck at sunset on Saturday, ramming a gate with a suicide car bomb and following up with a sustained onslaught against one of the most symbolic targets in Iraq. Apache helicopters and infantry reinforcements repulsed the attack after about 40 minutes, leaving at least one insurgent dead, according to a US military spokesman, who said the engagement was a defeat for the resistance.*

# Mon 04-Apr-05

Psalm 94:1-3
*O, LORD God, to whom vengeance belongeth; O, God, to whom vengeance belongeth, shew thyself.*
*Lift up thyself, thou judge of the earth: render a reward to the proud.*
*LORD, how long shall the wicked, how long shall the wicked triumph?*

I was walking to my trailer last night and I was talking to God about some things that I had seen going on. I felt that something had to be done about a certain issue that was really ruffling my feathers. I didn't get an answer. I felt like I was crying out like David was. It is interesting then that I read this Psalm this morning. Vengeance is the Lord's alone. Verse one says it twice that vengeance belongs to God. No matter what I might want to happen to someone God says that vengeance belongs to him. God will be the one to decide when the time has come for his wrath to fall. Until then we must be patient and know that God was patient with us as well. His want and desire is that all men will repent and come to Him. So in return our desire should be the same thing.

**Thought for the day:** Think of where you could have been except for the Father's saving grace, and then pray that your enemy will find Jesus' Saving Grace.

## Tue 05-Apr-05

Ephesians 5:25-27, 31
*Husbands, love your wives, even as Christ also loved the church, and gave himself for it;*
*That he might sanctify and cleanse it with the washing of water by the word,*
*That he might present it to himself a glorious church, not having spot or wrinkle, or any such thing; but that it should be holy and without blemish.*
*For this cause shall a man leave his father and mother, and shall be joined unto his wife, and they two shall be one flesh.*

"Marriage... Marriage is what brings us together today." This is one of my favorite lines from the Princess Bride, but is fits perfectly here today. For many years now the definition of marriage has become muddied by the world. Marriage was a union between a man and a woman. Now the world is trying to change that. Marriage was for life. Now divorce is second nature. The percentage of divorce per first time marriage is steadily on the rise. What is really amazing is that the percentage of second and third marriages ending in divorce is even higher. Marriage is not a commitment all it is a way to some benefits while you are living with someone.

This is not what God wanted. When he created man and woman he had a specific plan in mind. His plan was that man would leave his father and mother and cleave to his wife. I see so many people that once they get married their parents still want to control their life. The daughter or son goes back home when there is a fight. The parents feel rejected when the son or daughter wants to spend time with the new family. All of this is understandable but there are times when marriages must have time to grow and mature. The couple must be able to work through the problems that might arise.

When a couple gets married the wife must be the apple in her husband's eye. She must be his favorite. The relationship between the mother and her son has now changed and his wife is now in the limelight. Husbands need the prince for every wife. He will sweep in and care for the wife forever. The relationship must be built on honesty and integrity, filled with communication and above all else, to use another word from the Princess Bride, ("To blathe" which meant, "True Love").

## Wed 06-Apr-05

Matthew 4:18-20
*And Jesus, walking by the sea of Galilee, saw two brethren, Simon called Peter, and Andrew his brother, casting a net in to the sea: for they were fishers.*

*And he saith unto them, Follow me, and I will make you fishers of men.*

*And they straightway left their nets, and followed him.*

When Jesus was choosing his disciples he didn't go to the wealthy or the smart. He went to the lowly fishermen. He saw them and was encouraged by what they were doing. Being a fisherman was not an easy job. There were many long days of fishing when they would not catch anything. You had to not only be patient but also be persistent to be a fisherman. Jesus wanted someone with that type of tenacity and persistence. I really love what he tells them though, Follow me and I will **MAKE** you fishers of men. He didn't tell them that they would be become fishers of men, because that would imply that they had done something. Jesus said the he would **MAKE** them. This implies that Jesus would train them and mold them into fishers of men.

Then the disciples followed Him with blind faith and reckless abandon. They left their nets. They could have told Him, Hey, let us put these up real quick. Instead they left what they were doing and followed Him.

Jesus wants us to be fishers of men as well. He will mold us and make us if we are willing to just stand up and get started. We must have the faith to just start, then he will do the rest. Maybe you are already started and feel that God is putting you in places that you don't want to be. These times are when He is "making" you. You must be willing to allow God to put you in places so that he can mold you appropriately.

**Thought for the day:** If you take the first step he will take you the rest of the way.

## Thu 07-Apr-05

1 Peter 2:13-16

*Submit yourselves to every ordinance of man for the Lord's sake: whether it be the king, as supreme;;*

*Or unto governors, as unto them that are sent by him for the punishment of evildoers, and for the praise of them that do well.*

*For so is the will of God, that with well doing ye may put to silence the ignorance of foolish men:*

*As free, and not using your liberty for a cloak of maliciousness, but as servants of God.*

When you come in the Army you promise to support and defend the constitution and that you will obey the orders of the President and the officers. Sometimes the decisions that they make I might feel like are not the best decisions but I need to still submit myself to them and do what they say. This is the way it is throughout life. If we don't obey the orders of those put in authority over us what type of witness are we being to them.

Many people feel that they must disobey the laws of the government to prove a point.

The only point that it proves it that Christians are disobedient. It truly hurts the witness that God wants us to be.

When we are driving and decide to speed because we need to get to church, what type of witness are we? We must consider the effects of our decisions that we make and ensure that we submit to those in authority.

**Thought for the day:** What if we are the only way that the leader will see God, how will they see Him today?

# Fri 08-Apr-05

Psalm 138:1-3

*I will praise thee with my whole heart: before the gods will I sing praise unto thee.*

*I will worship toward thy holy temple, and thy name for thy lovingkindness and for thy truth: for thou hast magnified thy word above all thy name.*

*In the day when I cried thou answered me, and strengthened me with strength in my soul.*

As a child I was always reminded to say thank you to people for things that they had done for me. If I got a present, I said thank-you. If someone held the door open I said thank-you. It got to the point that I never had to be told to say thank-you any more. Now as a father I constantly tell my children the same thing. It is always important to say thank-you. It shows that we are grateful for what has been given to us.

When we pray to God for certain things do we ever remember to praise him for answering our prayer? Do we thank Him for bringing us through our problems? Do we praise him for providing for our needs? I know that it is harder to say thank-you to God for things than it is to tell a human thank-you. God wants to hear that he is appreciated just like we do. Let's try to tell Him today just how much He is appreciated.

*BAGHDAD, Iraq -- The second year anniversary of the collapse of Saddam Hussein's which originally happened in a matter of hours as much of Baghdad came under American control. Across much of the capital, Iraqis took to the streets to topple statues of Saddam, loot government ministries and interrogation centers, and give a cheering, often tearful welcome to advancing American troops.*

# Sat 09-Apr-05

Philippians 1:27-30

*Only let your conversation be as it becometh the gospel of Christ: that whether I come and see you, or else be absent, I may hear of your affairs, that ye stand fast in one spirit, with one mind striving together for the faith of the gospel;*

*And in nothing terrified by your adversaries: which is to them an evident token of perdition, but to you of salvation, and that of God.*

*For unto you it is given in the behalf of Christ, not only to believe on him, but also to suffer for his sake;*

*Having the same conflict which ye saw in me, and now hear to be in me.*

In High School I was not one of the jocks. I was probably considered to be a "geek." But more importantly I was one of those "Christian Geeks." I didn't cuss, party, drink, or do anything that all the jocks did. I tried to live my life as I thought Christ wanted me to. One day I had enough of one of the guys at school. He had been disrespectful to one of the teachers and I wasn't going to take it anymore. I started arguing with him and before I knew I had cussed him out and almost gotten in a fight with him. Then it hit me, what type of witness had I become?

In the verse for today, Paul instructs us to be careful of what our conversation is. It needs to build up the gospel of Christ. If we are complaining all the time, or swearing all the time, or gossiping all the time we are not building up the gospel of

Christ. Those against the gospel of Christ are looking for Christians to slip. They want to call us hypocrites. It is Satan's desire to ruin Christ's gospel and run people away from the light. We must be able to counter that with words of purity and truth. Let us remember that no matter what Christ is always there watching you and hearing what you are talking about. "Strive today for the faith of the gospel."

## NEWS OF THE DAY
### Sat 09-Apr-05

*BAGHDAD, Iraq -- A militant group said that it had kidnapped the deputy of the Pakistani charge d'affaires in Baghdad, Malik Muhammad Javed, who disappeared on Saturday. A separate group said it had captured and executed Basem Mohammed Kadem, a brigadier general in the Iraqi army. Tens of thousands of supporters of the radical Shia cleric Moqtada al-Sadr rallied in Baghdad on Saturday, the second anniversary of Saddam's fall, to demand an end to the US-led occupation.*

# Sun 10-Apr-05

Psalm 112:1
*Praise ye the Lord. Blessed is the man that feareth the LORD, that delighteth greatly in his commandments.*

Many people feel that Christians are goody two shoes. They don't have any fun and will never live their life to the fullest. This verse is an exciting promise. If we fear the Lord and delight in his promises then we will be blessed. Now that blessing is not only a current, in this life, blessing; it is also a blessing for everlasting life. It is a wonderful life that cannot be compared to anything that the world has to offer. There are many times though that we as Christians fall back into what the world wants us to be doing and when we do that we are turning our back on God's commands. As we live our life let us strive to live it for Him.

# Mon 11-Apr-05

Acts 1:8
*But ye shall receive power, After that the Holy Ghost is come*
upon you:
*And ye shall be my witnesses unto me both in*
*Jerusalem.And in all Judea, and in Samaria, And unto the*
*uttermost part of the earth.*

One of the most amazing things happened at the concert
the other night. I never would have expected it and neither did any of
the other Charlie Daniels fans. In the middle of the concert, Charlie
sang a gospel song and dedicated it to his Lord and Savior Jesus
Christ. What amazed me was not that he sang the song, because
anyone can sing a song. What amazed me was the fact that he
dedicated to Jesus. It took a lot of guts to say that in front of a lot of
soldiers.
Many soldiers today don't want to tell others about their
relationship with Jesus because they feel that they will be ridiculed.
There is a feeling of fear whenever they are put on the spot and asked
who they love. There was an old song that the Christian Artist,
Carmen, used to sing called "Who do you love?" The answer was
yelled out "JESUS". We are supposed to be the witness for Christ
where ever we are; whether that is in the United States, Afghanistan,
or Iraq. So tell me "WHO DO YOU LOVE?"

# Tue 12-Apr-05

2 Timothy 2:8-10
*Remember that Jesus Christ of the seed of David was*
*raised from the dead according to my gospel:*
*Wherein I suffer trouble, as an evil doer, even unto bonds;*
*but the word of God is not bound.*
*Therefore I endure all things for the elect's sakes, that they*
*may also obtain the salvation which is in Christ Jesus with*
*eternal glory.*

Here is Paul. He is writing to Timothy from prison. He is

telling Timothy and us to remember Jesus when we are feeling persecuted. We will suffer pain for the gospel. Satan doesn't want the Gospel to go forth. When it goes forth then people turn from their wicked ways and follow Christ. We must endure even through times of pain and agony. When people defame you, endure. When people gossip about you, endure. It is not for you that you endure, it is for Christ and those who seek Him. Endure!

## Wed 13-Apr-05

Ecclesiastes 5:15
*As he came forth of his mother's womb, naked shall he return to go as he came, and shall take nothing of his labour, which he may carry away in his hand.*

There was a commercial on television the other day and it showed a man hiding his money under his mattress. The commercial was talking about how we should save for the future. It said that we shouldn't do it like that man but actually put in a bank or in investments. realized then that the priority for many people is that they must have money to be happy. The realization though as we do save our money and plan for the future is this: We can't take it with us. Everything that we are saving will be left here. There is nothing that we can do to convince God that we should be able to take what we have earned with us to the other side of heaven.

With that said, the time that we have on this side of heaven we need to be content in what God has given us and not spend our whole life trying to make more money. I have seen so many families that never see the parents because they are trying to earn that next big promotion. They are trying to earn enough money so that they can keep up with the Joneses. So as they are doing that, their family is suffering. Their priorities are all askew. Instead of looking out for the real best interest of their family, they are trying to provide monetarily. Most kids when asked whether they want a lot of stuff or their parents would say that they want their family. Where are your priorities? If they are not in line with God's, you might want to reevaluate them.

# Thu 14-Apr-05

Deuteronomy 8:17
*And thou say in thine heart, my power and the might of mine hand hath gotten me this wealth.*

The old saying, "Pride cometh before a fall" is a great lead-in for a discussion of this verse. Man in his self-centered, egotistical nature has found a way to take the credit for everything that God has done. Even now there are scientists that have cloned animals and are trying to clone humans. Once they have done that then they can that they are god. There are many people in this world that fail to give God the credit for what He has done. It is not by man's hands that human life originates. God gives us the ability to work and the ability for our employer to pay us. It is God's desire that we be happy and satisfied in what we have been given. We should learn from the Israelites of old. God took care of their needs and they were still ungrateful. Then they became proud of their accomplishments and God had to humble them. Let us repent of our ways before it is too late and God has to humble us.

## NEWS OF THE DAY
Thu 14-Apr-05

*BAGHDAD, Iraq -- Two suicide car bombings killed at least 15 people and wounded around 20 during rush hour in Baghdad today, ministry and hospital officials said. The explosions happened near an Iraqi interior ministry building in the centre of the city. Around 200 metres apart, the bombs detonated in quick succession on a busy street, destroying cars and leaving debris strewn over a wide area.*

# Fri 15-Apr-05

Job 5:17-18

*Behold, happy is the man whom God correcteth: therefore despise not thou the chastening of the Almighty:*

*For he maketh sore, and bindeth up: he woundeth, and his hands make whole.*

As a child, I always seemed to get into trouble. I truly hated the punishment and sometimes felt that the punishment didn't fit the crime but I always was happy to get a hug from my parents when it was done and know that they loved me. I knew that when I had done something wrong that I deserved punishment. I was glad when I felt the love that came with it. There are times when we as parents discipline our children and fail to let them know how much we do love them. Our heavenly Father chastens us because He loves us. Sometimes we as parents are too caught up in the moment and want to make a point to our children that we react out of anger rather than love. We must understand that God, when he punishes us will also bind up our wounds. He will make them better. When we punish our children sometimes we take it too far and we can't fix it. Let us follow God's example and correct our children in love.

# Mon 09-May-05

Judges 2:10-11

[10]*And also all that generation were gathered unto their fathers: and there arose another generation after them, which knew not the LORD, nor yet the works which he had done for Israel.*

[11]*And the children of Israel did evil in the sight of the LORD, and served Baalim:*

I was in church the other day and had the opportunity to hear about a young lady who has taken a stand for her faith. She was told that she couldn't wear a Christian T-shirt to school. After her parents sought legal counsel she was allowed to wear the shirt. This young lady didn't care what other people in her generation were doing or what they thought, she was going to take a stand and live for Christ. Here is a young lady who could have just as easily backed down and decided that she could be a quiet Christian. It would be a whole lot easier. She wouldn't be looked at weird. Instead she took a stand for Christ. If people in our generation will not take a stand then who will? I once heard someone say that Christianity is one generation from extinction. How true this is. If we don't take a stand and tell others about Christ then who will? Let us take a stand today.

## Tue 10-May-05

Acts 22:3-4, 14-15

*³I am verily a man which am a Jew, born in Tarsus, a city in Cilicia, yet brought up in this city at the feet of Gamaliel, and taught according to the perfect manner of the law of the fathers, and was zealous toward God, as ye all are this day.*

*⁴And I persecuted this way unto the death, binding and delivering into prisons both men and women.*

*¹⁴And he said, The God of our fathers hath chosen thee, that thou shouldest know his will, and see that Just One, and shouldest hear the voice of his mouth.*

*¹⁵For thou shalt be his witness unto all men of what thou hast seen and heard.*

I recently bought a guitar. I was so excited to be finally able to have a good sounding guitar that I could play praise and worship songs in bible study and in chapel service while I was in Iraq. My wife and I had discussed whether I needed a hard case for it or whether the soft gig case would protect it while it was on the plane. We finally decided that it should be okay because most of the airlines have the protective boxes that I could put something fragile in. (I haven't flow commercial airlines in a while) Needless to say they couldn't take care of the case but I took my chances. Upon arrival in Iraq I found out that my guitar had been damaged. It is still playable but it is not in the good condition that it once was.

How true it is in life. When God created us he created us

for a purpose. That purpose was to glorify him with our talents, whatever they may be. As we progress through our life we many times become damaged because of the world that we live in. We fall into Satan's grasp and we become damaged. God still wants to be able to use us no matter what condition we are in. He will take us just like he took Paul and made him a great man of God. Will you let Him take control of your life today? He can use you just as you are.

---

## NEWS OF THE DAY
### Tue 10-May-05

*BAGHDAD, Iraq -- Insurgents who control parts of the western Iraqi desert appeared to have fallen back to regroup as the Marines prepared a new assault on a force of more than 200 fighters hiding or roaming the towns and desert in the remote areas just east of the Syrian border, a Marine commander said today.*

# Wed 11-May-05

Zechariah 7:9-14

*⁹Thus speaketh the LORD of hosts, saying, Execute true judgment, and shew mercy and compassions every man to his brother:*

*¹⁰And oppress not the widow, nor the fatherless, the stranger, nor the poor; and let none of you imagine evil against his brother in your heart.*

*¹¹But they refused to hearken, and pulled away the shoulder, and stopped their ears, that they should not hear.*

*¹²Yea, they made their hearts as an adamant stone, lest they should hear the law, and the words which the LORD of hosts hath sent in his spirit by the former prophets: therefore came a great wrath from the LORD of hosts.*

*¹³Therefore it is come to pass, that as he cried, and they would not hear; so they cried, and I would not hear, saith the LORD of hosts:*

*¹⁴But I scattered them with a whirlwind among all the nations whom they knew not. Thus the land was desolate after them, that no man passed through nor returned: for they laid the pleasant land desolate.*

I remember, as a child how hard headed I was. There were times that my parents would try to tell me how I needed to do something and I would shrug them off and do it my own way. I remember on many occasions that I found out the hard way that they were right and I was wrong, but I still didn't listen to their guidance. God in his infinite wisdom has given us some guidance. That guidance has been given through His word. So many of us still try to ignore what He has said and go our own way. We think that we know what is best for our lives. How can God know what is best for us? He isn't here, having to live in the world that we live in. Our world has become a self-indulgent world. Everything is about living for #1. Because we refuse to listen to what God has to tell us then our hearts are being hardened. It is like we are putting ear plugs in our ears so that we don't hear what God has to tell us, but those plugs are on the ears to our heart. May we repent and ask God to soften our heart before He has to go to extreme measures to get our attention.

---

NEWS OF THE DAY
Wed 11-May-05

*BAGHDAD, Iraq -- At least 71 people are killed and more than 160 wounded as suicide bombers rip through a crowded market and a line of security force recruits in a wave of explosions and gunfire across Iraq.*

## Thu 12-May-05

Psalm 46:1-7, 10-11
*¹God is our refuge and strength, a very present help in trouble.*

*²Therefore will not we fear, though the earth be removed, and though the mountains be carried into the midst of the sea;*

*³Though the waters thereof roar and be troubled, though the mountains shake with the swelling thereof. Selah.*

*⁴There is a river, the streams whereof shall make glad the city of God, the holy place of the tabernacles of the most High.*

*⁵God is in the midst of her; she shall not be moved: God shall help her, and that right early.*

*⁶The heathen raged, the kingdoms were moved: he uttered his voice, the earth melted.*

*⁷The LORD of hosts is with us; the God of Jacob is our refuge. Selah.*

*¹⁰Be still, and know that I am God: I will be exalted among the heathen, I will be exalted in the earth.*

*¹¹The LORD of hosts is with us; the God of Jacob is our refuge. Selah.*

When do people turn to God the most? It is when He seems the furthest away. He is our refuge. A refuge is a place that we can go to hide away and

out the storm. Ships go to an inlet or bay that keeps the waves down during a storm to protect the boat. That inlet is a refuge for that boat. We seek refuge indoors when there is a storm outside as well. I received some pictures recently of a gigantic sand storm that came to an undisclosed location here in Iraq recently. The person who took the picture said that as the storm approached he sought refuge indoors until it blew over. It is the same way it is with other devastating things that happen in our lives. Many times when we lose dear friends or loved ones to death we must seek refuge in our heavenly Father. He will protect us and comfort us. Though questions arise we must be still and allow God to comfort us. Seek comfort in Him today.

---

NEWS OF THE DAY
Thu 12-May-05

*BAGHDAD, Iraq -- Insurgents killed 12 people in a suicide car bombing at a crowded Baghdad marketplace and assassinated two top Iraqi security officials, the latest incidents in an escalation of bombings and ambushes.*

# Fri 13-May-05

Psalm 55:4-6, 16-19, 22
*⁴My heart is sore pained within me: and the terrors of death are fallen upon me.*

*⁵Fearfulness and trembling are come upon me, and horror hath overwhelmed me.*

*⁶And I said, Oh that I had wings like a dove! for then would I fly away, and be at rest.*

*¹⁶As for me, I will call upon God; and the LORD shall save me.*

*¹⁷Evening, and morning, and at noon, will I pray, and cry aloud: and he shall hear my voice.*

*¹⁸He hath delivered my soul in peace from the battle that was against me: for there were many with me.*

*¹⁹God shall hear, and afflict them, even he that abideth of old. Selah. Because they have no changes, therefore they fear not God.*

*²²Cast thy burden upon the LORD, and he shall sustain thee: he shall never suffer the righteous to be moved.*

Many of you know that earlier this week 327ᵗʰ Signal Battalion was hit hard by the loss of one of our own. There are so many unanswered questions. Why would God allow a young man to die? Why would he allow two young children to lose the father? These questions won't be answered here on earth. We are all in mourning. Some of us are angry and want revenge. Others are afraid to travel on the roads that we traveled on before. It is at this time that we must call upon the name of the Lord. He will save us. He will give us a peace that will go beyond all measure. We must cast our cares on Him. He will see us through. It is God's goal to see us strengthened through this. When troubles come upon us we must call on the name of the Lord. He will give us peace and rest. Just call on HIM!

---

### NEWS OF THE DAY
### Fri 13-May-05

*BAGHDAD, Iraq -- In the past 24 hours alone, at least five US soldiers have been killed and more than a dozen injured. Four of those soldiers were killed near the Syrian border where US troops have encountered stiff resistance since launching an offensive there a week ago. Several car bombs exploded in Baghdad, with the worst killing 17 people in the east of the capital.*

# Sat 14-May-05

Titus 3:3-7

*³For we ourselves also were sometimes foolish, disobedient, deceived, serving divers lusts and pleasures, living in malice and envy, hateful, and hating one another.*

*⁴But after that the kindness and love of God our Saviour toward man appeared,*

*⁵Not by works of righteousness which we have done, but according to his mercy he saved us, by the washing of regeneration, and renewing of the Holy Ghost;*

*⁶Which he shed on us abundantly through Jesus Christ our Saviour;*

*⁷That being justified by his grace, we should be made heirs according to the hope of eternal life.*

The best example of mercy that I have ever heard of is when a state governor pardons a man who is on death row. At times that pardon takes place literally hours before he is supposed to be killed. That person in that prison has had no opportunity to show anyone outside the prison that he is a changed person. There is literally nothing that can be done by that individual who is on death row that will change his sentence. Someone else must intervene on his behalf. It is the same way with our spiritual life. We are all sitting on death row. We can't do anything that will get our sentence reduced. The verdict was read...Death. Now it is up to the Father to intercede on our behalf. What is amazing is that he has already interceded. All we have to do is accept the fact that God showed grace and sent His son to replace us on death row. There he died. He died to pay for my sins. He wanted to be able to have me join Him in heaven someday. So many people though won't accept that fact that He died for them. Instead they think that they must live and die on Death Row. But Christ came that we might live not die. Won't you allow Him to take your place? It will be the best decision that you have ever made.

# Sun 15-May-05

Joshua 1:1-3, 9

*¹Now after the death of Moses the servant of the LORD it came to pass, that the LORD spake unto Joshua the son of Nun, Moses' minister, saying,*

*²Moses my servant is dead; now therefore arise, go over this Jordan, thou, and all this people, unto the land which I do give to them, even to the children of Israel.*

*³Every place that the sole of your foot shall tread upon, that have I given unto you, as I said unto Moses.*

*⁹Have not I commanded thee? Be strong and of a good courage; be not afraid, neither be thou dismayed: for the LORD thy God is with thee whithersoever thou goest.*

How would you feel if you just found out that your boss had just died? Here was the strongest spiritual leader that Joshua had ever known. What was Joshua supposed to do? God told <u>him</u> to take the lead. Everyone from the tribes of Israel would be looking at Joshua for not only spiritual leadership, but also military leadership. They will be looking for his guidance. What an intimidating position. Then you hear God tell him that all of the promises that he made to Moses he would fulfill in Joshua. To me it would be a very humbling position for me. Then God told Joshua the most comforting thing. He said He would be with him no matter where he went.

There are many times in our life that it seems like we are doing things on our own. We feel like we are fighting the battles by ourselves. God just doesn't seem present. Well, during those times we must turn to Him and cast our cares on Him. He will take care of us. He will see us through. We must stay in His will and He will bless beyond all measure.

Thought for the day: Are you facing a battle that seems unbearable? Turn to God and He will see you through.

# Mon 16-May-05

Joshua 6:1-5

*¹Now Jericho was straitly shut up because of the children of Israel: none went out, and none came in.*

*²And the LORD said unto Joshua, See, I have given into thine hand Jericho, and the king thereof, and the mighty men of valour.*

*³And ye shall compass the city, all ye men of war, and go round about the city once. Thus shalt thou do six days.*

*⁴And seven priests shall bear before the ark seven trumpets of rams' horns: and the seventh day ye shall compass the city seven times, and the priests shall blow with the trumpets.*

*⁵And it shall come to pass, that when they make a long blast with the ram's horn, and when ye hear the sound of the trumpet, all the people shall shout with a great shout; and the wall of the city shall fall down flat, and the people shall ascend up every man straight before him.*

There are many things that God wants us to do that we just don't understand. Here are Joshua and the Israelites who are preparing for war. God tells them to walk around the city. Now, how unconventional is this. I wonder if Joshua was thinking, "Lord, I really need to be preparing battering rams and catapults to get us over the walls." Instead God wanted them to just march around the city. He was showing them that what they were about to do wasn't in their own power but in His alone. I wonder if Joshua had told the elders that God had told them to walk around the city, but he thought it was crazy, if God would have blessed. The thing that we must be able to do is trust God enough to allow him to work in our life. I know so many people that have physical ailments. Sometimes all God wants from them, before He will heal them, is for them to reach out and ask Him to help them. When they ask Him it is a sign of trust. We must truly trust God and He will bless beyond all measure. I have been trying to lose some weight for quite a while. I have been trying to do it in my own power. Sometimes the physical battles that we have are rooted in a spiritual problem. I felt God tugging at my heart the other day and telling me to give this weight problem to Him. I now have to trust Him. This is hard, but it must be done. It is easier to pray for others and their needs rather than my own. May I always trust Him with my needs as well.

Lord, take my life and use it for your glory. I trust you and know that you have a great plan for my life. Amen,

---

NEWS OF THE DAY
Mon 16-May-05

*BAGHDAD, Iraq -- The bodies of 38 men shot execution-style were found dumped around an abandoned chicken farm, a trash-strewn lot and an insurgent stronghold west of the capital, police said Sunday. This is the latest in an endless stream of violence, much of it designed to destabilize Iraq's new government and hasten a US retreat. More than 450 people have been killed in just over two weeks since Prime Minister Ibrahim al-Jaafari's Cabinet was announced. At least 10 more Iraqis were killed in a spree of bombings and shootings Sunday.*

# Tue 17-May-05

Psalm 57:1-4
*¹Be merciful unto me, O God, be merciful unto me: for my soul trusteth in thee: yea, in the shadow of thy wings will I make my refuge, until these calamities be overpast.*

*²I will cry unto God most high; unto God that performeth all things for me.*

*³He shall send from heaven, and save me from the reproach of him that would swallow me up. Selah. God shall send forth his mercy and his truth.*

*⁴My soul is among lions: and I lie even among them that are set on fire, even the sons of men, whose teeth are spears and arrows, and their tongue a sharp sword.*

In the past week there have been a lot of things going on. I am feeling like I am being overwhelmed with so many things that are being thrown at me. First of all we lost a soldier due to enemy attack. Then I find out that one of my wife's childhood friends is having extreme medical problems and is not sure how long she has to live. Then my Grandmother takes a fall and ends up in ICU for bleeding on the brain. I say all of this because it is at times like this that we must learn to trust in the Lord. As the Psalmist writes: "Yea,, in the shadow of thy wings will I make refuge, until these calamities be overpast." God is here not only as a judge of the earth, but even more as one who wants to provide refuge for us. We must be able to trust God enough though to take refuge in Him. Trusting God with our problems is extremely hard at times, but He will take care of you if you just release your problems to Him.

Thought for the day: Can you trust God enough with your problems and allow Him to take the stress off of you

---

NEWS OF THE DAY
Tue 17-May-05

*BAGHDAD, Iraq -- Mortars, bombs and drive-by gunmen killed at least 24 Iraqis, and the new government Monday vowed to capture and punish the killers of at least 50 other people found slain in the past 48 hours, charging that insurgents were trying to start open warfare between the country's Shiite majority and Sunni minority. Two car bombs exploded within minutes at a mostly Shiite Baghdad market, killing at least nine soldiers and a civilian in a rash of attacks many here worry could deepen the conflict beyond the deadly insurgency against US forces and their Iraqi allies.*

# Wed 18-May-05

2 Chronicles 1:7-10
   [7]*In that night did God appear unto Solomon, and said unto him, Ask what I shall give thee.*

   [8]*And Solomon said unto God, Thou hast shewed great mercy unto David my father, and hast made me to reign in his stead.*

   [9]*Now, O LORD God, let thy promise unto David my father be established: for thou hast made me king over a people like the dust of the earth in multitude.*

   [10]*Give me now wisdom and knowledge, that I may go out and come in before this people: for who can judge this thy people, that is so great?*

147

My daughter is graduating from K-5 this Friday and I am so proud of her. Every year at my children's school the K-5 students do a play as a part of their ceremony. I am looking forward to hearing what this year's is about. My daughter was born in the Ukraine and has been having to learn the English language this past year as well as adjust to a different way of life. My desire for her though is that she will not only gain the wisdom that it will take for her to succeed in the world but more importantly that she will gain Godly wisdom. It is through Godly wisdom that she will be able to truly be able to conquer the battles of life.

When God asks you what you want, what do you tell Him? Is it health, wealth, or happiness? Ultimately all of these things will pass away. Solomon was a very wise man. He had just taken over as King of Israel. I imagine he was just a little overwhelmed. He did the best thing that could be done. "Lord, please give me wisdom and knowledge, that I may go out and come in before this people..." Solomon express a want for anything except knowledge and then the wisdom to how to use the knowledge properly. This should be our desire as well.

Lord, may we have just an inkling of knowledge that you gave Solomon and the wisdom to use it properly. Amen.

## Thu 19-May-05

Matthew 5:13
*13 Ye are the salt of the earth: but if the salt have lost his savour, wherewith shall it be salted? it is thenceforth good for nothing, but to be cast out, and to be trodden under foot of men.*

When I was a kid I used to watch my father salt his food. He loved salt. It added to the flavor of the food. When I tasted it though I thought that it was almost bitter. I liked just a pinch of salt on some food maybe but very rarely would I put any on my food. Each person has a different tolerance for salt.

As I have been studying this verse over the past six months I have always been intrigued by the fact that Jesus called us to be salt of the earth. I would compare it to tenderizing a piece of meat. Yesterday, though I realized that too much salt can ruin a piece of meat as well. I was confronted by someone who is tired of hearing people talk about Jesus. He has been blasted by "religion" and just doesn't want to hear it. As I am trying to be the salt I must realize that sometimes people need a lot to be tenderizing and others need just a little bit. May we always be sensitive to the needs of others and not just try to push Jesus on them.

## Fri 20-May-05

*Read Acts 10-11*

Acts 11:1-4, 17-18
*¹And the apostles and brethren that were in Judaea heard that the Gentiles had also received the word of God.*
*²And when Peter was come up to Jerusalem, they that were of the circumcision contended with him,*
*³Saying, Thou wentest in to men uncircumcised, and didst eat with them.*
*⁴But Peter rehearsed the matter from the beginning, and expounded it by order unto them, saying,*
*¹⁷Forasmuch then as God gave them the like gift as he did unto us, who believed on the Lord Jesus Christ; what was I, that I could withstand God?*
*¹⁸When they heard these things, they held their peace, and glorified God, saying, Then hath God also to the Gentiles granted repentance unto life.*

Peter has just come from the house of Cornelius the Centurion. Cornelius was a Roman, thus he was a Gentile. The Jews hated the Gentiles. The Gentiles were considered unclean people and the Jews were considered clean. To be caught eating with someone that was unclean was unthinkable. Once Peter told his story of how God had cleansed the Gentiles and that these people had received the Holy Spirit then everyone realized that God had given them the gift of salvation as well.

There are so many "Christians" that won't go out and minister to those that are lost. Instead they expect that someone else will do it or that if God wanted that other individual saved then He will save them without their help. Other Christians feel that they are "too good" to get down in the gutters and minister to these people. Notice I didn't say get these people saved. We as Christians cannot save people. No matter how hard we try to save an individual, we won't be able to do it. God is the one who saves that individual. So many Christians get caught up in numbers of people who got saved that they forget about ministering to those individuals. Sometimes ministering to these people means living in the trenches with them. It could mean taking them somewhere they want to go even if you don't want to go there. We must be able to step out of our comfort zone and go to where the people are. If we don't get off of our high horse and get down in the trenches with the unlovable then how will they ever see Christ? We are his messengers. Will we wait for people to come to us or will we go to them?

## Sat 21-May-05

Ecclesiastes 5:10
*10 He that loveth silver shall not be satisfied with silver; nor he that loveth abundance with increase: this is also vanity.*

In 1994 I joined the Army. I was content with my meager paycheck of $900 Dollars a month. In fact that was the most money that I had ever made. I also realized that I was on a fixed income. There would not be any increase until the next year. But I knew that I had a set paycheck coming in so I was guaranteed that certain amount. Soon I was living out of my means. I would try to rationalize what I was doing by the fact that I would be getting this certain amount of money on the first or the fifteenth of the month. I was living from paycheck to paycheck. In fact I knew when the money would hit the bank and when I could write a check without bouncing it. Before long I was so far in debt that I couldn't see out. It has taken years of work (and God isn't done yet) for me to realize that I need to be satisfied with where I am.

Being satisfied with what I have is not something that is easy to do. "He who has the most toys when he dies wins" seems to be the push for many people. We often forget that we can't take what we have with us. As I was reading Ecclesiastes this morning I was reminded of that. A couple of days ago I heard a rumor that the hazardous duty pay for the military was going to be going up to $750/month. This is an increase of $500. I got really excited. Then I realized something. This money is for soldiers, who are separated from their families, in a combat zone. I realized that yes the money would be nice, but my family is much more important than money could ever be. We must put things in perspective and realize that money will not buy happiness. Instead, if we love money then we won't ever be satisfied with what we have.

May we be satisfied with what we have, and when God gives us increase may we praise Him for it and not look for more.

## Tue 24-May-05

Psalm 90:12
*12So teach us to number our days, that we may apply our hearts unto wisdom.*

When I was a child, I knew a boy who had some physical ailments. He was a hemophiliac, that is his blood didn't clot, and he had some other physical disfigurements. This young man was a great guy though. I met him at church. There were days when he couldn't come to Sunday school because he had to have a platelet transfusion. One day I found out that he had died. He was nine years old. I couldn't understand why God would let someone die at such an early age. It wasn't until recently that I began to understand that we all have our days numbered. Some will live longer than others. When Adam and Eve sinned, there was the curse of death placed on all mankind. We all will die sometime. What matters is what we do with our life while we are living. Sometimes we feel that we will live forever but then we realize that life is just too short. May we understand that our days are numbered, and let us begin to do things that will count for eternity.

# Wed 25-May-05

*Read 1 Samuel 17:31-52*

1 Samuel 17:48-51
*[48]And it came to pass, when the Philistine arose, and came, and drew nigh to meet David, that David hastened, and ran toward the army to meet the Philistine.*
*[49]And David put his hand in his bag, and took thence a stone, and slang it, and smote the Philistine in his forehead, that the stone sunk into his forehead; and he fell upon his face to the earth.*
*[50]So David prevailed over the Philistine with a sling and with a stone, and smote the Philistine, and slew him; but there was no sword in the hand of David.*
*[51]Therefore David ran, and stood upon the Philistine, and took his sword, and drew it out of the sheath thereof, and slew him, and cut off his head therewith. And when the Philistines saw their champion was dead, they fled.*

David was a young man. He was probably about the age of 12-15 years of age. This Philistine was a giant. David probably was not even full grown. As the Israelites quaked in their boots David made plans to defeat this giant. David knew that the God of Israel would take care of him and would give him victory. It is very interesting though, as the Giant is preparing for battle and getting all of his armor put on, David goes and picks up some stones. David was going to use the weapon that he knew. He didn't try to use a weapon that was not familiar to him.. Once David knocked the giant down he could have been all excited and bragged about what he had done but instead he went and finished the job. He drew the Giant's own sword and killed him.

We all have many battles that we face daily. Some of those battles are self-inflicted; others are life battles. How we deal with those battles is what is really important. There are times when it is wise to take a sword into battle, but other times you might need to take a sling and five smooth stones. I think that it is very interesting how David didn't take Saul's sword and gear because he had not "proved them". In the military we never go into battle without going to the range to ensure that our weapons are tested and zeroed. David took the weapon that he knew even if it was not theoretically smart. Sometimes we must be different to accomplish our goals. God will help us, just as He did with David, but we must be willing to be face the giants in our life. Once we have knocked down our giants we must finish them off. Are you willing to face the giants in your life? How will you fight them? Will you allow God to help you overcome them or are you going to try to beat your giants on your own? You are being called to action. What will you do?

---

NEWS OF THE DAY
Wed 25-May-05

*BAGHDAD, Iraq -- U.S. forces launched a wide-ranging offensive Wednesday against insurgents in western Iraq, involving about 1,000 American and Iraqi troops in Sunni-dominated Anbar province.*

# Thu 26-May-05

Proverbs 31:10-12
*[10] Who can find a virtuous woman? for her price is far above rubies.*
*[11] The heart of her husband doth safely trust in her, so that he shall have no need of spoil.*
*[12] She will do him good and not evil all the days of her life.*

When God created Eve, He knew what He was doing. He created her to be a helpmate for Adam. When Adam looked at Eve, he thought she was the most beautiful thing in the whole world. I believe that God smiled down and was pleased. The book of Proverbs speaks of how a virtuous woman should be. Here it talks not only about how much she is worth but it says how trustworthy she is. This is the type of wife that every man wants to have. Today is the anniversary of my wedding. As I sit in the desert thousands of miles away from my wife, I know that I trust her. She and I are one. The road has not always been easy but through the grace of God, He has seen us through. My wife is far more valuable to me than

153

anything that is on this earth. I praise God for her.

This message in scripture wasn't just written for those who were married. It is also for those who are seeking a wife or those who are a woman seeking a husband. Gentlemen seek a wife who is righteous and honest. Seek a woman whom you can trust. And most of all start praying now for your spouse.

Lord, Thank you for my Spouse. May she always be virtuous and trustworthy. AMEN.

---

NEWS OF THE DAY
Thu 26-Jul-05

*BAGHDAD, Iraq -- The Iraqi government announced a huge counter insurgency operation in the capital yesterday, with 40,000 troops being deployed on the streets within the next week to stop the attacks that have killed more than 650 people in the past month. In the biggest operation to date involving the country's fledgling forces, soldiers and security officers are throwing a security cordon around the capital and manning 675 checkpoints.*

# Fri 27-May-05

*Read Philemon*

Philemon 1:8-9
*[8] Wherefore, though I might be much bold in Christ to enjoin thee that which is convenient,*
*[9] Yet for love's sake I rather beseech thee, being such an one as Paul the aged, and now also a prisoner of Jesus Christ.*

Nobody likes being told what to do. Here is Philemon, who is a slave owner, and Paul, who is imprisoned. They both have something in common, a relationship with Onesimus. To Philemon, he is a slave that has run away. To Paul, he is a new brother in Christ. Paul wanted Philemon to welcome Onesimus back with open arms as a brother in Christ, rather than a runaway slave. What is very interesting about this letter from Paul is not how Paul is sending Onesimus back to Philemon, but rather how Paul speaks to him. Paul is extremely tactful. In fact, the way that Paul is speaking to

Philemon is almost as if he is asking for compassion on a his son or brother. Through Paul's authority he could have easily told Philemon that he had to take Onesimus back. If Paul had done this, Philemon probably would have gone on the defensive and things would have gone bad. Instead Paul was gracious and tactful.

I don't know how many times in my life I have heard that I need to think before I say something. Either what I say is not tactful or it is inappropriate. As a leader it is sometimes easier to just tell someone what to do rather than influence them in their decision making process. Sometimes it is better if the person you are talking to feels like they have come up with the idea on their own. They feel like they are contributing to the team rather than always being told what to do. Influencing others to accomplish the mission is paramount. Paul's ability to do this set a great example for others to follow. May we all learn from him.

## Sat 28-May-05

Colossians 1:20-23

*20And, having made peace through the blood of his cross, by him to reconcile all things unto himself; by him, I say, whether they be things in earth, or things in heaven.*

*21And you, that were sometime alienated and enemies in your mind by wicked works, yet now hath he reconciled*

*22In the body of his flesh through death, to present you holy and unblameable and unreproveable in his sight:*

*23If ye continue in the faith grounded and settled, and be not moved away from the hope of the gospel, which ye have heard, and which was preached to every creature which is under heaven; whereof I Paul am made a minister;*

Recently I was talking to a person who couldn't understand how God could forgive them of the things that they had done. This person was a Christian. He had just fallen away from God and gone his own way. I told him that once you have asked for forgiveness for that sin and repented from it then God has thrown it away. What that individual was experiencing was self-incrimination. He was continuously beating himself down for what he had done rather than praising God for the forgiveness and grace that He has given. God's grace is never ending. No matter how far we fall away from God, He will never let us go.

If you are in this situation, God wants to commune with you. He will forgive you, but you must ask with a repentant heart. God will give you the strength to turn from your sin. You feel that you will be alienated forever from God because of your sin, but He will reconcile you. Turn to Him today!

---

NEWS OF THE DAY
Sat 28-May-05

*BAQUBAH, Iraq -- Two American soldiers were killed when their helicopter was shot down by insurgents near Baqubah.*

# Sun 29-May-05

Matthew 28:5-7
*⁵And the angel answered and said unto the women, Fear not ye: for I know that ye seek Jesus, which was crucified.*

*⁶He is not here: for he is risen, as he said. Come, see the place where the Lord lay.*

*⁷And go quickly, and tell his disciples that he is risen from the dead; and, behold, he goeth before you into Galilee; there shall ye see him: lo, I have told you.*

I was participating in taking the Lord's Supper this morning and something was impressed on me. So many times when I prepare my heart for worship or the Lord's Supper, I visualize Jesus on the cross. As I was thinking about that today the realization came to me that He is not there. He was taken down off the cross and placed in the grave, where three days later He rose. We always hear that we need to go and place our sins at the cross. Well, Jesus is not on the cross or in the grave. He is alive! Our prayers for forgiveness should be to our Living Lord. He wants us to bring our sins to Him so that He can forgive them. Yes, Jesus died for our sins but He didn't stay there. I imagine that as I bring my sins to Him that He winces as He remembers the pain, and then He shows me the nail holes in his hands and says "I died for that one, too". Jesus doesn't have to continue dying for our sins. He already died for them and our sins have been paid for. We must be willing to live our life for Him though and repent and turn from our sin. Let us not continue to live in sin, but strive to live a righteous life for Him.

Lord, please help me to remember that you already died for me. Thank you for taking my sin and throwing it as far as the east is from the west. Help me live for you today. Amen.

## Tue 31-May-05

Micah 7: 7, 8
*[7] Therefore I will look unto the LORD; I will wait for the God of my salvation: my God will hear me.*

*[8] Rejoice not against me, O mine enemy: when I fall, I shall arise; when I sit in darkness, the LORD shall be a light unto me.*

"When life gives you a sour pickle, get some peanut butter". Sometimes in life we feel that nothing can go right. When I was in Highschool, I met a young man who was not all that coordinated. It was as if he had not quite grown into his feet. There were times when he would trip over his feet and sometimes fall. One day in the lunch room I saw him trip and really bust it. If I had been in his shoes I would have run away and hid because it was very embarrassing. Instead of running away, this young man jumped to his feet and said, "And for my next trick I will do..." and he proceeded to do something else. This young man had some peanut butter to eat with his sour pickle.

There are going to be days when life just doesn't seem to be going the way you want it to. It is at times like that when we should be comforted that God will hear our cry. So many times when we fall our enemy wants to make sure that we are truly down. They make fun of us and laugh at us. They even go for our weak points to ensure that we are really down. Take courage that God is there and He will comfort us. It is not His will for us to sit in darkness. He will light our way. All we have to do is call on Him.

# -FIELD NOTES-
*for Journaling*

# JUNE 2005

# Wed 01-Jun-05 08:27

Matthew 5:43-44
*⁴³Ye have heard that it hath been said, Thou shalt love thy neighbour, and hate thine enemy.*
*⁴⁴But I say unto you, Love your enemies, bless them that curse you, do good to them that hate you, and pray for them which despitefully use you, and persecute you;*

Praying for your enemy is an extremely hard thing to do. Here your enemy is telling all these evil things about you and doing bad things to you and Jesus tells us that we must pray for him. That is certainly not something I would want to do. In the book of Acts, Luke writes of a young man who did just this. His name was Stephen. He was preaching the good news of Jesus Christ. The Religious leaders didn't approve and decided to stone him. As Stephen was being stoned, he prayed that God would forgive the people that were stoning him. He could have easily prayed that God would cause them to die or be hurt, but instead he took a Christ like approach and prayed for them.

Loving our enemies is an extremely hard task but it is something that Jesus wants us to do. Today make a point to pray for someone who really gets on your nerves and see what God will do.

# Thu 02-Jun-05 09:21

Micah 2:10
*¹⁰Arise ye, and depart; for this is not your rest: because it is polluted, it shall destroy you, even with a sore destruction.*

I have been deployed in both Afghanistan and Iraq. In comparison between the Afghanistan deployment and Iraq deployment, I would take the Afghanistan deployment over this one. The reason for that is because we actually lived harder there. We slept in tents, ate in tents and showered in much worse conditions than we are here. What is happening here is we live in trailers, shower in trailers and eat in a nice dining facility. We can eat as much food as we want, and we even have Baskin Robbins ice-cream. We work in actual buildings rather than a wooden shell that we threw up to keep the sun and heat off of us. We have AC that actually works. We must be careful to not become so complacent that we forget that we are in a war zone. The reality of life is that the enemy would love to catch us with our guard down and then attack us.

This is the way it is in our spiritual life as well. We are not of this world. Although we were born here we will someday leave, either by death or by Christ coming back and calling us home. We should never become so comfortable living in this world that we don't look forward to going to our home in heaven. Before we go to that home, though, we do have a mission here on earth to do. Christ has called us to tell others about Him. If we become so accustomed to living in this world that we act like the world, then what type of witness are we? We must live here as lights for others to follow. In the end though we must be ready to leave this place and go to a much more glorious place that we call home.

---

NEWS OF THE DAY
Thu 02-Jun-05

*BAGHDAD, Iraq -- Three separate suicide car bombings killed 20 people in northern Iraq today, including a senior council leader and one of the bodyguards of Iraq's Kurdish deputy prime minister, officials said. In the deadliest attack, at least 12 diners were killed and at least 40 wounded in a big explosion targeting a restaurant this morning in Tuz Khormato, a town 55 miles south of the northern city of Kirkuk, the Iraqi defence ministry said. Colonel Abbas Mohamed Amin, chief of Tuz Khormato police, believed the suicide bomber, who was driving a white Toyota car, was following a group of bodyguards working for the deputy prime minister, Rowsch Nouri Shaways.*

# Fri 03-Jun-05 10:13

2 Corinthians 12:7-10
*⁷And lest I should be exalted above measure through the abundance of the revelations, there was given to me a thorn in the flesh, the messenger of Satan to buffet me, lest I should be exalted above measure.*

*⁸For this thing I besought the Lord thrice, that it might depart from me.*
*⁹And he said unto me, My grace is sufficient for thee: for my strength is made perfect in weakness. Most gladly therefore will I rather glory in my infirmities, that the power of Christ may rest upon me.*
*¹⁰Therefore I take pleasure in infirmities, in reproaches, in necessities, in persecutions, in distresses for Christ's sake: for when I am weak, then am I strong.*

Have you ever received a test? Does it always seem to come when you feel everything is going just right? We have had some trying times recently. There has been an escalation in attacks around us. The other day there was a huge explosion near us and I rushed outside to see what was going on. I thought that it had happened in our living areas. I immediately began to ask God why he allowed something to happen within our borders. I have been praying that God would keep the rockets and mortars outside of our perimeter. Well this was a test again as the boom was outside the gate. God is telling me that I should understand that He is in charge. His strength is made perfect in my weakness.

Lord, build your strength because I am definitely weak.

## Sat 04-Jun-05 09:21

Romans 1:9
*For God is my witness, whom I serve with my spirit in the gospel of his Son, that without ceasing I make mention of you always in my prayers.*

Recently I was talking to my brother who has 4 children. His son and now two of his daughters pray for "Uncle Eric, who is in the Army" every night. It is such a comfort to know that little ones are praying for me continuously. I have received other letters that say that they are praying for us while we are in harm's way. I think that it is important that we lift each other up continuously. This should be done, not as an obligation, but as a blessing. Not only should those who are in harm's way be lifted up, but we need to lift up all fellow believers. It is important that we pray for each other without ceasing.

Let us think of each other daily and continuously lift each other up in prayer.

## Sun 05-Jun-05 11:26

Over the years I have heard numerous different preachers speak on Jesus' saving grace. They talk about how Jesus came to die for our sins so that we might be able to live eternally with Him. The interesting thing was that each pastor taught it in a different way. I have heard some almost scare you into heaven. Others tend to plead with you to get saved. Others still just tell you how it is and leave it at that. Recently I was brought under conviction that sometimes we as believers try too hard to win the lost that we run them away from the cross. This verse speaks volumes to that. It says that we should show compassion to some and in doing this we will make a difference in their life for eternity. Others we might have to scare to keep them out of hell. One of those Preachers was a man by the name of Jonathan Edwards. (I didn't hear him preach. I just read one of his sermons.) One of his most famous sermons was titled "Sinners in the Hand of an Angry God". What a way to get his listener's attention. Each one of us has the opportunity to share with others who are lost. We must listen to the Holy Spirit's guidance and He will help you through it. The most important thing though is that we be willing to be used and God will do the rest.

## Mon 06-Jun-05 09:16

1 John 2:28-29

*28And now, little children, abide in him; that, when he shall appear, we may have confidence, and not be ashamed before him at his coming.*

*29If ye know that he is righteous, ye know that every one that doeth righteousness is born of him.*

When I was growing up I was a little bit on the rambunctious side. I would get into trouble and my parents would have come and pick me up from school for cutting up in class. I remember that I got suspended from school one day for hitting another boy. As I was sitting in the principal's office, I was not only scared but I was ashamed that my parents were going to come and see me here. I really wanted to be good but I just couldn't. I was ashamed to be a Scheidt and be in this kind of trouble.

If we abide in Christ and live the way that He wants us to live then we won't have to be ashamed for the way we have acted when He comes back. Many people that I talk to want to know why we have to do good things. They say, "If being a Christian is not a works oriented faith then why should I do good things?" The answer is right here. We don't want to be ashamed of our actions, when Jesus returns. He wants us to love Him and not "do" things for Him but instead he wants us to live our life for Him. We are what the world sees. If we are living as the world does then what will make them want to turn to Christ. If Jesus was righteous, then we need to strive to be righteous as well. Again it is not something that we "do" but it is a lifestyle change.

Challenge for the day: Ask Jesus to make you righteous and He will show you what needs to be worked on in your life.

## Tue 07-Jun-05 11:31

Romans 6:18
*Being then made free from sin, ye became the servants of righteousness.*

When the settlers came to America they were seeking "Freedom." Many settlers could not afford their passage on the ships so they became servants for wealthy people who lived in the Colonies. These settlers would work the land to repay their debt. Most were happy to do it though because they were still free. They were free from the tyranny of England. But their freedom was bought with a price.

Our freedom from death and sin was bought with a price. That price was Christ's blood. Christ made us free from sin. Because we are free from sin we have become servants of righteousness. This is kind of confusing. Why would we want to be a servant to something if we had been just been made free? The interesting thing is that we only have two choices. Be a slave to sin or a servant to righteousness. As a servant you have the choice of what you do. As a slave you don't. I think that it would be wiser to be a servant to righteousness rather than a slave to sin. If you are a slave you must be bought out of it. There are many people who continue to be slaves to sin because they don't realize that the price has been paid already for them. As a slave on the auction block must go with his new master so must we go with Christ. He has already paid the price. All Jesus asks for you to do is to step down off the block and come <u>serve</u> Him. It is your choice. It is a choice that will last for eternity.

---

## NEWS OF THE DAY
### Tue 07-Jun-05

*BAGHDAD, Iraq -- Insurgents in Iraq ended a brief spell of peace yesterday with a wave of attacks that killed at least 19 people and wounded dozens more. Four bombs exploded in and around the town of Hawija in the space of seven minutes in a coordinated assault on Iraqi security forces and US troops. The detonation of a roadside bomb appeared to be the signal for three suicide car bombers waiting in lines of traffic at checkpoints to blow themselves up, killing six Iraqi soldiers and 13 civilians and wounding 39 others.*

# Wed 08-Jun-05 08:43

Luke 9:57-62
*⁵⁷And it came to pass, that, as they went in the way, a certain man said unto him, Lord, I will follow thee whithersoever thou goest.*
*⁵⁸And Jesus said unto him, Foxes have holes, and birds of the air have nests; but the Son of man hath not where to lay his head.*
*⁵⁹And he said unto another, Follow me. But he said, Lord, suffer me first to go and bury my father.*
*⁶⁰Jesus said unto him, Let the dead bury their dead: but go thou and preach the kingdom of God.*
*⁶¹And another also said, Lord, I will follow thee; but let me first go bid them farewell, which are at home at my house.*
*⁶²And Jesus said unto him, No man, having put his hand to the plough, and looking back, is fit for the kingdom of God.*

When new recruits for the Army get ready to ship off to Basic training, they go to a processing station. While they are there they say the oath of enlistment. Once that has been said there is no turning back. There is no going back home to Mom and Pop. They leave from the processing station and go to the airport or bus station to be shipped off to Basic Training. While in Basic there is no contact from family members except for phone calls. All of this is done to instill a dependence on each other, rather than on family members.

In today's scripture Jesus was not trying to be coarse when he said "Let the dead bury the dead." He was trying to let them understand that the life as a disciple would not be easy. At times your only family members would be those who were with you. Jesus wants us to leave what we are doing and follow him with no strings attached. This doesn't mean that we leave our current job, unless you feel he is leading you that way. What he truly wants for you to do is follow him with your spirit, mind and body. This will mean that you will have to leave some things behind. It will mean that you have to put self aside. All of the selfish ideals that we have must be put aside never to be picked up again. We shouldn't turn and try to pick up what we had before, once we have followed Christ. We can't serve two masters so we must choose whom we will serve. If you will follow Christ then you must put aside everything that is keeping you from following him wholeheartedly. Only then will you truly be following Christ.

## Thu 09-Jun-05 09:28

2 Chronicles 29:5-6

*5And said unto them, Hear me, ye Levites, sanctify now yourselves, and sanctify the house of the LORD God of your fathers, and carry forth the filthiness out of the holy place.*

*6For our fathers have trespassed, and done that which was evil in the eyes of the LORD our God, and have forsaken him, and have turned away their faces from the habitation of the LORD, and turned their backs.*

How many people look at their parents and say I will never be like them, but they end up like them? Johnny wants to place the blame on his parents for how he is acting now. Have you heard, "My dad was an alcoholic, and that is why I am"? Have you heard, "My mom was a druggy, so I am"? We all place the blame on our parents. I heard recently, "My parents made me go to church and they were such hypocrites, why would I want to go and become like that?" Again, this individual was blaming his lack of action because of his parent's actions. When will we take responsibility for our own actions?

In today's scripture, King Hezekiah realized that the people of Israel were not living for God. He said, "I know our fathers have done wrong and turned away from the Lord but it is time for us to turn out lives back to God." Never before is there a more dire time for us to realize that we must repent as King Hezekiah and the children of Israel did. We can no longer place the blame on others. We must repent from our wicked ways. If your parents led you down the road of destruction today, you can get out. Jesus is reaching down and wants to pull you out. Will you let Him do that today?

---

NEWS OF THE DAY
Thu 09-Jun-05

*BAGHDAD, Iraq -- American diplomats and army commanders have held indirect talks with insurgents in Iraq, the first officially sanctioned contact between the two sides in two years of violence. A US embassy official in Baghdad said efforts were under way to "engage" elements of the resistance in an apparent softening of the Bush administration's opposition to negotiations.*

# Fri 10-Jun-05 10:00

Amos 6:1
*Woe to them that are at ease in Zion, and trust in the mountain of Samaria, which are named chief of the nations, to whom the house of Israel came!*

The saying, "Complacency Kills" is more apparent than ever before. There are so many people that feel that we are safe here. We jokingly call the base where I am Fort Bragg Forward. This is a base where we eat in a nice Dining Facility. We have a choice of 6 of Baskin Robbins' 31 flavors of ice cream. We do physical training on a regular basis. We live in trailers. We work in Air Conditioned offices. We lose the reality that we are in a dangerous place. People don't have the awareness that right on the other side of the wall there are people that want us dead.

What about people's spiritual life? How many churches are filled with people that are there just because it is a habit for them to be there? Where is their relationship with God? So many times we as Christians become complacent in our spiritual life. We live our lives like we are guaranteed tomorrow. Therefore we can always talk to God tomorrow. God wants to communicate with us everyday. With me being deployed I miss talking with my wife so I try to call her on a regular basis. God wants to have a relationship with us. He wants to talk to us. He wants to laugh when we laugh and comfort us when we are sad. He has initiated the relationship, now we must respond. Don't let your complacency kill your spiritual life.

## Sat 11-Jun-05 08:43

Amos 7:14-15
*14 Then answered Amos, and said to Amaziah, I was no prophet, neither was I a prophet's son; but I was an herdman, and a gatherer of sycamore fruit:*
*15 And the LORD took me as I followed the flock, and the LORD said unto me, Go, prophesy unto my people Israel.*

Imagine being in the fields watching over sheep and a voice comes to you calling you to minister to God's people. What would you do? This happened to a number of people in the Old Testament. It happened to Moses, David, and Amos to name a few. I wonder why God picked herdsman or shepherds to take care of His people. I think that it was probably because these men had proven themselves in the small things. Here are men who have been shepherds all of their lives. They have to know where all of their sheep are. They are responsible for the well being of the sheep. This is to include where the sheep eat, drink, and sleep. They must ensure that they are protected from everything that is evil. I think that when God looked down on these shepherds He saw himself as well. He knew what was going to happen. He would be called the Good Shepherd. He would search after any lost sheep. And ultimately He would have to lay down his life for his flock. This was His calling.

Are you being responsible in the little things that you have to do? Does God look down at you and say, "Now there is someone that I want to use for something bigger"? Will you be willing to go no matter what the cost? Will you be willing to answer when God calls? God has a job for you but you must be ready and that means being faithful in the little things.

## Sun 12-Jun-05 08:41

Colossians 2:8
*Beware lest any man spoil you through philosophy and vain deceit, after the tradition of men, after the rudiments of the world, and not after Christ.*

We must be very cautious as believers not to fall into the trap that the Devil has placed. It is his goal that the people of God will be deceived and turn against what they believe. As the end of the world draws near there are going to be many people that feel that there should be a world church. This world church will be one that encourages every one of all faiths to join together and be one. I was talking with someone the other day that believes that Jesus is **a** way to Heaven. He thinks that God in his infinite power could allow all these other religions to provide variety in life and that they each provide a way to Him. This man and I did not see eye to eye on this issue. In today's verse, Paul warns us to be very careful to test all philosophy. If it is not of Christ then it is deceitful and wrong. Jesus says in John 14:6, I am the way, the truth, and the life: no man cometh unto the Father, but by me. We must ensure we follow Christ and not after man.

177

# Mon 13-Jun-05 09:00

Psalm 13:1-6

*¹How long wilt thou forget me, O LORD? for ever? how long wilt thou hide thy face from me?*

*²How long shall I take counsel in my soul, having sorrow in my heart daily? how long shall mine enemy be exalted over me?*

*³Consider and hear me, O LORD my God: lighten mine eyes, lest I sleep the sleep of death;*

*⁴Lest mine enemy say, I have prevailed against him; and those that trouble me rejoice when I am moved.*

*⁵But I have trusted in thy mercy; my heart shall rejoice in thy salvation.*

*⁶I will sing unto the LORD, because he hath dealt bountifully with me.*

Have you ever had one of those days? Things are just not going your way? King David can vouch for that. Many of David's Psalms were written while he was hiding from, the king at the time, King Saul. David's prayer is that of a broken and lonely man. He says where are you God? Why can't I feel you here? How long will I have to talk to my self and comfort myself? David is almost having a pity party, but then he makes a drastic move to get out of the mood. He says, "I trust you." David understands that God allows things to happen for a reason. Then he praises God for being faithful and dealing well with him.

Now what can we learn from this? We all have times when we wish that we could just curl up in a ball and never get up. In the movie, "It's a wonderful life", George Bailey was at wits end. He needed a touch from God, but first he had to learn a lesson. The angel Clarence came down to talk to him and George told Clarence that he wished he had never been born. This was a man who was truly at depressed. Before long George realized the impact that he had in everyone's life in his town. He finally realized that his life was worth living. There are some days when we all have these feelings. We just don't understand what our purpose here. At those times we must learn to look at what God has done in our life and allow Him to comfort us. Sometimes we will be comforted by the least likely of people, but we will be comforted if we allow God to do it.

Will you trust God and allow Him to comfort you today?

---

NEWS OF THE DAY
Mon 13-Jun-05

*KIRKUK, Iraq -- A man wearing a belt packed with explosives blew himself up outside a bank in northern Iraq Tuesday, killing 23 people and wounding nearly 100, including child street vendors and pensioners waiting for their checks. In Baghdad, the bodies of 24 men killed in ambushes were brought to a hospital. A car bomber also rammed his vehicle into an Iraqi army checkpoint, killing five soldiers and wounding two others in Kan'an, 30 miles north of Baghdad, Iraqi army Col. Ismael Ibrahim said. Two civilians also were wounded in the attack claimed in an Internet posting by the Ansar al-Sunnah Army affiliated with Al Qaeda in Iraq.*

## Tue 14-Jun-05 09:11

Joel 2:12-13
*[12]Therefore also now, saith the LORD, turn ye even to me with all your heart, and with fasting, and with weeping, and with mourning:*
*[13]And rend your heart, and not your garments, and turn unto the LORD your God: for he is gracious and merciful, slow to anger, and of great kindness, and repenteth him of the evil.*

What is true repentance? Is it running around with a sad face, saying woe is me? Is it paying a lot of money to an organization or church for them to take your sins away? For many people it is telling someone, "I am sorry for..." But is this really repentance? In the Old Testament times a person showed their repentance for something by tearing their clothes. They would put on sackcloth and would put dust on their head and would fast and pray. This was a great outward sign for what should have been happening on the inside. Many of us do the same thing today. We make a big show about how bad we feel that we did something, but nothing has changed on the inside. Joel writes, "Rend your heart, not your garments, and turn unto the LORD your God." True repentance

179

shows a change in heart. Your heart must be truly broken. Once repentance happens in your heart, then there will be a change on your exterior as well. Is it time to truly repent and change something in your life? Take it to the Lord today.

## Thu 16-Jun-05 10:34

Daniel 7:18
*But the saints of the most High shall take the kingdom, and possess the kingdom for ever, even for ever and ever.*

Watching and playing with my kids is the highlight of my day. I love to wrestle with them. A couple of years ago my son and I would play on the trampoline and I would chase him around and around it. We would play steamroller. He would just giggle and laugh as he would try to stay away from me. It was so much fun. We were so happy. When I thought that we were going to be moving to Germany, I sold the trampoline. We don't experience that joy that we did then anymore.

Soon we will all be in the Kingdom that God has prepared for us. It will be an awe inspiring time. We will be so happy to be in our Heavenly Father's presence. I imagine Him playing with us and enjoying watching us enjoy the Heaven that has been prepared for us to live in. What is amazing is that we will have it forever. That means all of eternity. It will never be taken away from us. We will never outgrow it. I imagine that God will continue to surprise us for all of eternity. What a day that will be when we go and see what He has prepared for us. Are you ready to go? Are you ready to experience joy for eternity?

NEWS OF THE DAY
Thu 16-Jun-05

MUSAYYIB, Iraq -- *A suicide bomber targeted a marketplace in Musayyib, Iraq. The attacker detonated his explosive belt in the crowded marketplace, where hundreds of people had come to shop and mingle after the day's stifling heat subsided. The attack happened as a tanker containing cooking gas was*

*passing, triggering an inferno that destroyed dozens of buildings, including a*
*nearby Shiite mosque.*

# Fri 17-Jun-05 09:35

Daniel 9:17-19

*[17]Now therefore, O our God, hear the prayer of thy servant,*
*and his supplications, and cause thy face to shine upon thy sanctuary*
*that is desolate, for the Lord's sake.*

*[18]O my God, incline thine ear, and hear; open thine eyes, and*
*behold our desolations, and the city which is called by thy name: for we*
*do not present our supplications before thee for our righteousnesses, but*
*for thy great mercies.*

*[19]O Lord, hear; O Lord, forgive; O Lord, hearken and do;*
*defer not, for thine own sake, O my God: for thy city and thy people are*
*called by thy name.*

Intercessory prayer is something that very few people do.
We all pray for our needs. We even pray for our family and our
friends. When was the last time that you prayed for your city, state,
or nation? Since I have been here in Iraq, I have prayed for the
physical safety of the base. There have been very few times, though,
that I have prayed for the spiritual security. It seems so hard to do
that. I just get caught up in what my needs are. You see, when I pray
for the physical security of the base, it is actually a prayer for me. If I
take the time to pray for the spiritual well being of those around me
think about how much better it would be.

I receive emails all of the time about what we need to do to
change our country. We need to sign this petition against stem-cell
research, or banning same sex marriage, or you name it I have
received it. I haven't seen where people ask you to pray for your
nation though. We are a nation of action. We must do something.
Maybe, what we really need to do is just pray for our nation. Let us
follow Daniel's example and pray. It is only through prayer that
revival will truly happen.

Lord, revive us again!

*BAGHDAD, Iraq -- American troops backed by warplanes and helicopters yesterday launched one of their biggest offensives in recent months to hunt insurgents on Iraq's border with Syria. About 1,000 marines with tanks and amphibious assault vehicles fanned across the desert near Karabila, a flashpoint town in Anbar province, following a spate of clashes in the area.*

## Sat 18-Jun-05 09:23

Hosea 6:1-3

*¹Come, and let us return unto the LORD: for he hath torn, and he will heal us; he hath smitten, and he will bind us up.*

*²After two days will he revive us: in the third day he will raise us up, and we shall live in his sight.*

*³Then shall we know, if we follow on to know the LORD: his going forth is prepared as the morning; and he shall come unto us as the rain, as the latter and former rain unto the earth.*

Revival comes in many different ways. I remember as a teenager we used to have a week of revival at my school. (I went to a Christian school). We would sit through an hour a day of some body preaching at us and telling us that if we didn't get our lives right with God that we were going to go to Hell. Many of the students would stand up as a sign of their repentance and then they would go back to class and do exactly what they had said they wouldn't do. On many occasions I would stand up just for show. There had not been any actual revival in my heart. I just wanted these people to get off of my back. There was this one preacher that was different. He wasn't yelling at us. He talked to us as if he was one of us. He talked about the life that he had lived. Then he talked about how God brought him to his knees. Then he talked about how God changed his life. This preacher was talking to us and sharing with a part of his life. He wasn't just shouting at us. God used his message to bring revival into that school.

What is it going to take for you to have revival in your life? The other day I wrote about repentance. True repentance works hand in hand with revival. In fact it is the beginning stage of revival. God doesn't want us to continue to live in this dark existence that we call life. He has a much better plan for us. We just must step in to the light and then we will be able to truly see what he has to offer. Just as it is refreshing to take a shower after a hard day at work, so it is when God comes forth into our life. He will refresh us and clean us from the inside out. True revival is not just repentance but also a renewal to live the life that Christ wants us to live. COME LET US RETURN TO THE LORD!

---

### NEWS OF THE DAY
Sat 18-Jun-05

*BAGHDAD, Iraq -- The U.S. military on Thursday reported the capture of a man described as al Qaeda's leader in the northern Iraqi city of Mosul. Air Force Brig. Gen. Donald Alston identified him as Abu Talha -- whose actual name is Muhammad Khalaf Shakar -- and said he was captured on Tuesday without a fight.*

## Sun 19-Jun-05 10:25

Ephesians 5:1
*Be ye therefore followers of God, as dear children;*

When I was much younger I believed everything that my parents told me. When they told me that Santa was real I believed it. I believed them when they told me that the Tooth fairy took my tooth and put it as a star in the sky. I was even convinced that if I swallowed watermelon seeds that they would grow out of my ears. Some people would say that children are so gullible. I would say that they just trust their parents. When Paul was writing to the Ephesians, this same childlike trust and faith is what we should have as followers of God. Adults are always analytical. They must always ask why they have to do something, before they do it. A child will just do it because they were told to. When adults follow God, they tend to pick apart why something happened, rather than just understanding that it was the will of God. If we could only have the faith of a child, then life would not be so complicated. Remember we are God's children and thus we must follow Him as a child. When we are adults, we wander off on our own, thinking that we can do things without God. Let us get back to that childlike faith, which we once had.

Lord, make me as a child once again, so that I can truly trust and follow you.

## Tue 21-Jun-05 09:01

Ecclesiastes 12:13-14
*13 Let us hear the conclusion of the whole matter: Fear God, and keep his commandments: for this is the whole duty of man.*
*14 For God shall bring every work into judgment, with every secret thing, whether it be good, or whether it be evil.*

Recently there has been a rampant usage of the phrase "coming out of the closet". It has been used for people who have decided to tell the world that they are living a homosexual lifestyle. Something similar to that phrase has been around for centuries. "What you do in secret God knows". You see, what man doesn't see, God sees. The things that we think man doesn't know about, God knows about. In today's scripture we see that God will bring every work into judgment. That is to include everything that has been done in secret or in the closet. When we look back at our lives how many things have we done that we really don't want the whole world to see? Have we been hiding things in the closet of our heart? Do we have skeletons that need to be done away with? If you are doing something that you don't want someone else to see, then it is probably something that you shouldn't be doing. God knows what is in our heart. He just wants us to follow his laws and live ur life for Him. Let us then fear God and keep his commandments. This isn't all that hard to do. Let us all focus on that today.

2 Corinthians 12:9

*And he said unto me, My grace is sufficient for thee: for my strength is made perfect in weakness. Most gladly therefore will I rather glory in my infirmities, that the power of Christ may rest upon me.*

Dads are so great! They let you do something on your own until you figure that you can't do it by yourself and then when you ask for help that is when they will step in and either do it for you or more importantly show you how to do it. This is the way it is with God. God knows that we have things that we just can't do. It could be trying to control your temper, or your mouth. It could be trying to overcome alcohol addiction or a drug addiction. It could be trying to keep your mind pure from sexual lusts. There are many different things that plague man, but God knows how to cure them. So many times we try to fix the problem on our own. We try the newest drug on the market to make us more laid back, but it doesn't work. We try a detox facility, which works for a while but there is always the desire for a drink. You try to put only good things in your mind, but everywhere you look there is something to lust after. What we really need to do is look to God. Cry out to Him for help. He will see us through our struggles into a permanent victory. When we ask Him for help we must be willing to give Him everything. We must be willing to be humble so that He may be lifted up. Turn you problems over to Him today and be free.

---

## NEWS OF THE DAY
Thu 23-Jun-05

*FALLUJA, Iraq --On Thursday night, a suicide car bomber struck a U.S. convoy in Falluja. The attack killed at least four Marines -- including three women, U.S. military sources said. Of 13 Marines wounded in the attack, 11 were female, the sources said. A Marine and a sailor remain unaccounted for. Their genders were not disclosed. It was the deadliest day for U.S. women in uniform since World War II, according to Pentagon statistics.*

# Fri 24-Jun-05 11:20

1 Corinthians 12:26
*And whether one member suffer, all the members suffer with it; or one member be honoured, all the members rejoice with it.*

When a military unit is deployed the unit takes on a different shape. We all become a big family. As a big family we look out for each other like brothers and sisters. Recently our unit has experienced many painful things. We have seen two soldiers killed in the last month, and in the last week we have seen five other soldiers injured by a mortar attack. As we are all part of this unit/family, anytime that one of our members falls it is painful for the rest of us. We all suffer when the team is broken. It is that way in the Christian body as well. When one of us is hurting then we all should feel the pain. When one of us is rewarded for something then we should all be happy. Let us all remember that we are part of a much bigger family.

# Sat 25-Jun-05 08:38

1 Corinthians 15:51-52
*51Behold, I shew you a mystery; We shall not all sleep, but we shall all be changed,*
*52In a moment, in the twinkling of an eye, at the last trump: for the trumpet shall sound, and the dead shall be raised incorruptible, and we shall be changed.*

The whole concept of the second coming is somewhat troubling to me. I want Jesus to come. I really do, but I also feel that there are things that I am supposed to do while I'm still here. The idea of leaving my family is disturbing as well. I have so much still that I want to do with them. One of the things that I must realize is that God wants to be first in my life. It is his desire that He be placed before my family, before the other desires of my heart. I discussed this with one of my friends recently. We talked about how it is hard to understand what God's plan is. It is just the fact that I am not ready to die or be called home. Hearing this many people would want to doubt my salvation.  The real reason for this desire is not that I don't believe, but that I feel there are many other people that I need to share with before I go.  I know that soon though we will be called to account for our life.  May God's grace be evident in my life as well as in the lives that I touch.

# Mon 27-Jun-05 10:28

Psalm 47
*¹O clap your hands, all ye people; shout unto God with the voice of triumph.*
*²For the LORD most high is terrible; he is a great King over all the earth.*
*³He shall subdue the people under us, and the nations under our feet.*
*⁴He shall choose our inheritance for us, the excellency of Jacob whom he loved. Selah.*
*⁵God is gone up with a shout, the LORD with the sound of a trumpet.*
*⁶Sing praises to God, sing praises: sing praises unto our King, sing praises.*
*⁷For God is the King of all the earth: sing ye praises with understanding.*
*⁸God reigneth over the heathen: God sitteth upon the throne of his holiness.*
*⁹The princes of the people are gathered together, even the people of the God of Abraham: for the shields of the earth belong unto God: he is greatly exalted.*

The Book of Psalms is an intriguing book into the life of worship.  I was reading in the *Purpose Driven Life* this morning about how our worship should not be a regurgitation of what someone else has said.  Instead it needs to be something that you feel from your heart.  The authors of the Psalms just spilled out their feelings to God.  It was a different type of relationship with God than I am used to.  I am used to a structured type of prayer.  What God wants from us, though is more of a heartfelt communication with Him.  When I hear my wife praying, it is as though God is sitting right there beside her listening to her problems. She tells him just how she feels. If she is angry then she lets Him know that she is angry. When she is sad, she cries and has no inhibitions about it.

This is the type of relationship that God wants us all to have with Him. He wants to know how we really feel about things. In comparison to people on earth who don't have the time to listen to our problems, God has all the time in the world to talk. What amazes me though is that I don't take the time to do it. Many people's prayers are short prayers that consist of asking forgiveness, asking for something and then saying amen. There is no real apparent communication. Look how the author of this Psalm talks to God. "¹O clap your hands, all ye people; shout unto God with the voice of triumph." It is in song format and he is praising God for who He is. This is something that is very difficult for me to do. I imagine that it is hard for many other people to do as well. God wants to hear our praise though. Let us praise Him in our own way today.

---

NEWS OF THE DAY
Mon 27-Jun-05

*BAGHDAD, Iraq -- Three suicide bombings targeting Iraqi military and police stations killed 15 police officers and 18 civilians Sunday in the northern Iraqi city of Mosul, U.S. military officials said. The attack capped a deadly weekend in Mosul, Iraq's third-largest city, where insurgent violence has flared periodically since November. Sixteen civilian laborers died Sunday morning in a blast in the parking lot of the Kasak army post, the U.S. military said. A bombing at a police post outside Mosul's Jamahoori Hospital killed five police officers, military spokesmen said. A bomb hidden under a pile of watermelons in a truck outside the al-Toob police station in western Mosul killed 10 police officers and two civilians, Iraqi police and U.S. military spokesmen said.*

## Tue 28-Jun-05 09:09

Psalm 128
*¹Blessed is everyone that feareth the LORD; that walketh in his ways.*

188

*²For thou shalt eat the labour of thine hands: happy shalt thou be, and it shall be well with thee.*

*³Thy wife shall be as a fruitful vine by the sides of thine house: thy children like olive plants round about thy table.*

*⁴Behold, that thus shall the man be blessed that feareth the LORD.*

*⁵The LORD shall bless thee out of Zion: and thou shalt see the good of Jerusalem all the days of thy life.*

*⁶Yea, thou shalt see thy children's children, and peace upon Israel.*

What kind of blessings do you want from the Lord? For many, in this materialistic world that we live in. we want something tangible. The expectation of many is that God will give us something that we can touch and see. In fact I went to conference once where these tangible blessings were the topic. The teacher was telling us that all we had to do was follow after God and we would become millionaires. We would be able to get anything that we wanted. God would bless us "with the desires of our heart". As I read today's scripture, this is not what this is talking about. The Bible says that we will be blessed. Verse two says that we will have enough food to eat, if we labour for it. God will bless us with children and grandchildren. If he blesses us with this he will also bless us with the ability to provide for them. All of these blessings will be given to us if we fear the Lord and walk in his path.

What does this mean? Walking in the path of the Lord is taking the harder right over the easier wrong. It is listening to Him and following His law. Most importantly it means having a relationship with Him. That is what God desires from us the most. He wants a relationship with us; one that goes past superficiality. It is one that lets God truly get into your heart and live with you. To use an analogy: God wants to be the driver of your life and not the backseat driver. Will you let Him drive your life today?

## Wed 29-Jun-05 09:45

Colossians 4:6
*Let your speech be alway with grace, seasoned with salt, that ye may know how ye ought to answer every man.*

When I was younger my mother would tell me to think before I spoke. When I got to my first duty station though I became a little more vocal about how I felt about things. I would express my feelings however I wanted to. I was told by one of my leaders that I had a right to say what I felt but that I must use tact when I was talking. It was interesting that if I would just speak with a little bit of grace, how much easier I would be received. I wish that I could say that I have overcome my tongue. If I had it would be much easier to write about this subject. We must all season our words with just a little bit of grace. It will always come across better. If I am trying to tell someone how to do something, it is accepted more readily if I use tact and grace. Now I strive to pass my words through Christ first. If it passes His test then I speak. Let us all speak words of grace to others.

## Thu 30-Jun-05 07:39

Job 16:7
*But now he hath made me weary: thou hast made desolate all my company.*

Have you ever just felt all alone? Growing up as the oldest of eleven and as a twin I never really felt alone until I left home and went to college. It was at that time that I really felt alone. I really didn't feel like I belonged. This is one of the reasons that so many people who leave home get into trouble with the wrong people. They feel like there is no one out there that will support them, so they try to find someone. Sometimes those friends are not the best type of friend. In Job's life he had three friends who came and sat with him while he was grieving. These friends really shouldn't have been called friends because all they did was discourage him even more. When he was down, they took him even lower. This is the way it is with people today, as well. When you are not feeling well emotionally, mentally or physically there are people that will continue to try to keep you down. Instead as believers we should lift each other up. There is a song that I love to listen to. The chorus says, "You raise me up, so I can stand on mountains..." This is what Christ will do for us. Man will fail you but Jesus will never falter. He will be your strength when you are down. All you have to do is cry out to Him, and he will see you through.

---

## NEWS OF THE DAY
### Thu 30-Jun-05

*BAGHDAD, Iraq -- According to the United States, to date, insurgent attacks in the last six months have killed more than 8,000 Iraqi civilians, police and troops, according to Iraq's interior minister. Meanwhile Thursday, a U.S. military spokesman in Baghdad said the insurgency's reliance on car bombs is due to their "high payoffs." In an interview with CNN, Iraqi Interior Minister Baqir Jabbur said "terrorists" had killed 8,175 people and wounded another 12,000 since January 2005.*

# -FIELD NOTES-
*for Journaling*

# JULY & AUGUST 2005

# Sat 02-Jul-05 10:21

1 John 4:7-10

*[7]Beloved, let us love one another: for love is of God; and every one that loveth is born of God, and knoweth God.*

*[8]He that loveth not knoweth not God; for God is love.*

*[9]In this was manifested the love of God toward us, because that God sent his only begotten Son into the world, that we might live through him.*

*[10]Herein is love, not that we loved God, but that he loved us, and sent his Son to be the propitiation for our sins.*

There was a song that we used to sing at camp many years ago called "They will know we are Christians" by Carolyn Arends. The lyrics talk about how Christians are unified in the Spirit and the Lord. They talk about how we will work well together. The most important thing that non-believers will see is, they will know that we are Christians by our love. Christ loved us and gave himself for us. This was the ultimate gift of love. All He wants us to do is love each other. Why is it then, that we see Christians hating other Christians? They destroy each other's reputations, and many times in doing so destroy their life. I think what happens is that we have succumbed to the world. We see how other people treat each other so we feel that we have to act as they do. We have forgotten what it means to truly love someone. We must remember that a tell-tale sign for being a Christian is how we love each other. We must love as Christ did.

**Thought for the day:** What have you done this week to show someone God's love?

---

## NEWS OF THE DAY
### Sat 02-Jul-05

*FALLUJA, Iraq -- When the roll call at Camp Falluja commenced on Friday, Marine First Sgt. John Forbes shouted six names. No one answered. The 400 troops mustered at the base's chapel then mourned amid deafening, heartbreaking silence.*

*Poignant moments marked the memorial service honoring and remembering five Marines and a sailor killed in last week's suicide attack in Falluja, six of the 1,741 troops killed in the war in Iraq. Three of the six were women -- Lance Cpl. Holly A. Charette, 21, of Cranston, R.I., Cpl. Ramona M. Valdez, 20, of the Bronx in New York, and Petty Officer 1st Class Regina R. Clark, 43, of Centralia, Wash. The others were men -- Cpl. Carlos Pineda, 23, and Pfc. Veashna Muy, 20, both of Los Angeles and Cpl. Chad W. Powell, 22, of West Monroe, La. All but Clark were Marines. But all were assigned to the 2nd Marine Expeditionary Force. Their comrades, shaken by the loss but emboldened by their associates' integrity, remembered them in prayer and personal reflection. The mode of the service wouldn't be unfamiliar to Americans. "Amazing Grace" was sung. "Eternal Father" -- a Marine prayer -- was recited. So were the 23rd Psalm and verses from Ecclesiastes.*

## Mon 04-Jul-05 09:17

Proverbs 25 9-12
*⁹Debate thy cause with thy neighbour himself; and discover not a secret to another:*
*¹⁰Lest he that heareth it put thee to shame, and thine infamy turn not away.*
*¹¹A word fitly spoken is like apples of gold in pictures of silver.*
*¹²As an earring of gold, and an ornament of fine gold, so is a wise reprover upon an obedient ear.*

These verses all talk about the words that we speak. Those words will either bring good or evil. In verse 9, the author is telling us not to gossip with others about someone. Instead we should tell the one whom we have a disagreement with what the problem is. If we gossip and talk about others we are not fixing the problem. Instead we have made ourselves out to be backbiters and fools. Many times I see myself thinking that I need to tell someone what is going on with someone else so that they can "pray" for them. This is also a form of gossip. Many churches have been divided up because of this very thing. I was reading in "The Purpose Driven life" this morning and the topic was this very thing. We as believers need to lift each other up. So many times we tear each other down because "I" want to look better. This is not what Jesus wanted.

Christ wanted us to be able to love each other enough that when there was something wrong in our life, our Christian brother or sister could confront us with grace and we would accept it. Right now, many people are too arrogant to accept the criticism or they are too proud and would rather not focus on their faults. We as believers must be humble enough to accept our faults. This goes for both the person who has done wrong and also the reprover. If the reprover is not humble when addressing the wrong in someone's life then the words that he uses will not be accepted. All in all, humility is the key to confrontation. God wants us to be wise with our words. When we are humble, we will be wise.

NEWS OF THE DAY
Mon 04-Jul-05

*BAGHDAD, Iraq -- Iraq has lost around $11.35 billion in damages to oil sector infrastructure and lost revenue since oil exports resumed after the war two years ago, an Iraqi oil ministry spokesman said Sunday. Assem Jihad said there were 300 acts of sabotage against Iraqi oil installations since Iraq resumed exports in June 2003 until May 31. He said 70 acts of sabotage took place in the first five months of 2005. Jihad said most of the sabotage took place in the northern oil installations preventing the country from exporting around 400,000 barrels a day from its northern oil fields via the Turkish port of Ceyhan.*

## Tue 05-Jul-05 09:48

Acts 1:7-8
*And he said unto them, It is not for you to know the times or the seasons, which the Father hath put in his own power.*
*But ye shall receive power, after that the Holy Ghost is come upon you: and ye shall be witnesses unto me both in Jerusalem, and in all Judea, and in Samaria, and unto the uttermost part of the earth.*

So many people want to know when Christ is coming back. Even the disciples questioned when Jesus would return and restore the Kingdom to Israel. Jesus' reply was that they were not supposed to know the time or the hour. They Father had it all under control. We just need to be His witnesses in all of the earth. I think that it is ironic that as I reading this I am in the uttermost part of the earth from my home. I am on the opposite side of the world from

202

everyone that I love and care about. The real question though is what I do with the time that I have in this part of the world. You see, I still have a choice of whether or not to be a witness for Him. I can choose to live my life as the world would want me to live it, or I can live it for God. This is a choice that I must make everyday. Jesus' command is to be a witness for him, but the choice is up to you. What type of witness will you be today?

---

## NEWS OF THE DAY
Tue 05-Jul-05

*BAGHDAD. Iraq -- Gunmen ambushed the top Bahraini and Pakistani diplomats in separate attacks as they drove through the capital today, spurring Pakistan to announce the withdrawal of its ambassador from Iraq. The Bahraini diplomat, Hassan Malallah al-Ansari, was struck in the right arm by a bullet and taken to a hospital. The Pakistani ambassador, Muhammad Yunis Khan, escaped unharmed, though a car in his convoy was raked by bullets. The ambushes came three days after the top Egyptian diplomat here was kidnapped as he drove alone through western Baghdad. Insurgents appear to have begun an organized campaign to drive Muslim diplomats out of Iraq as the American and Iraqi governments are pressing Arab countries to send ambassadors here and upgrade their diplomatic ties. The militant group led by Abu Musab al-Zarqawi, the Jordanian fighter, said in an Internet posting late today that it had kidnapped the Egyptian diplomat, Ihab al-Sharif. The message said Mr. Sharif had been abducted "by the hands of our mujahedeen, and he is under the control of the mujahideen." The group made no immediate demands.*

# Wed 06-Jul-05 09:46

Acts 2:16-21
*[16]But this is that which was spoken by the prophet Joel;*
*[17]And it shall come to pass in the last days, saith God, I will pour out of my Spirit upon all flesh: and your sons and your daughters shall prophesy, and your young men shall see visions, and your old men shall dream dreams:*
*[18]And on my servants and on my handmaidens I will pour out in those days of my Spirit; and they shall prophesy:*

*¹⁹And I will shew wonders in heaven above, and signs in the earth beneath; blood, and fire, and vapour of smoke:*
*²⁰The sun shall be turned into darkness, and the moon into blood, before the great and notable day of the Lord come:*
*²¹And it shall come to pass, that whosoever shall call on the name of the Lord shall be saved.*

When will the Lord come back? For years people have speculated. There are so many different answers. There are prophecies that must be completed, many of which already have been. The Lord has already poured out His Spirit on all flesh. There are people that see visions and dreams. Then there are things that will come to pass as a foreshadowing of the Lord's return. The most promising verse in this whole passage though is that whoever will call upon the name of the Lord shall be saved. That means the oldest and meanest person can be saved, if he calls on the Name of the LORD. God can save a murderer, rapist, liar, and a thief. God does not pick and choose whom He wants in heaven. If He did then we would have everyone there. Instead He gives us an option. Man was given free will. Through this will, we have the choice to decide if we want to be saved or condemned for eternity. That decision still rests in your hands. Call on Him today and choose LIFE!

## NEWS OF THE DAY
### Wed 06-Jul-05

*BAGHDAD. Iraq -- Task Force Baghdad soldiers said they have been overwhelmed and overjoyed by donations Americans have been sending to a program designed to provide school supplies, clothes and toys to Iraqi children. The "Iraqi Schools Program," founded by Army Maj. Greg Softy in August 2003, is currently being managed by soldiers of 3rd Battalion, 7th Infantry Regiment, 4th Brigade Combat Team, 3rd Infantry Division. Softy was the squadron operations officer with 1st Squadron, 1st Cavalry Regiment, 1st Armored Division, and has since rotated back to Germany.*

# Thu 07-Jul-05 11:08

Matthew 9:2-7

[2]*And, behold, they brought to him a man sick of the palsy, lying on a bed: and Jesus seeing their faith said unto the sick of the palsy; Son, be of good cheer; thy sins be forgiven thee.*

[3]*And, behold, certain of the scribes said within themselves, This man blasphemeth.*

[4]*And Jesus knowing their thoughts said, Wherefore think ye evil in your hearts?*

[5]*For whether is easier, to say, Thy sins be forgiven thee; or to say, Arise, and walk?*

[6]*But that ye may know that the Son of man hath power on earth to forgive sins, (then saith he to the sick of the palsy,) Arise, take up thy bed, and go unto thine house.*

[7]*And he arose, and departed to his house.*

What would you do if you were paralyzed and your friends took you to a miracle worker named Jesus? This, man in today's reading, must have been rather nervous, wondering if he would actually be healed. He had heard about this man they called Jesus. People were really talking Him up. There was the man who had been blind, but now he could see. There were those leprous fellows. Those guys were healed. Maybe this guy would have time for him. All he has to do is make me able to walk and move again. Then Jesus told the man that his sins were forgiven. I imagine the paralytic was thinking, "My sins forgiven? I didn't come here to get them forgiven. I came to be healed of my physical ailment." What if this was all that Jesus did? He could have left it at that; just forgiven the man's sins. Jesus understood though that there was a physical need as well as a spiritual need. Therefore he healed the man of both. What ailments do you have? Are they physical or are they spiritual? Jesus wants to heal them but you must have the faith to approach the throne and ask. What is holding you back? Are you worried that Jesus will see a sin that you don't want him to? Don't worry, he will forgive that too. He came to the earth and died for us to cover **all** of our sins. All we have to do is approach the throne and ask Him to heal us.

**Thought for the day:** What is holding you back from approaching the throne for total healing?

---

NEWS OF THE DAY
Thurs 07-Jul-05

*LONDON, England -- Bomb explosions tore through three London subway trains and a red double-decker bus in a deadly terror attack today, killing at least 37 people in coordinated rush hour carnage that left the city stunned, bloodied but stoic. Only one day after the British capital erupted in joy at winning the 2012 Olympic competition over such cities as Paris and New York, commuters packed in the city's subways - the Tube - were plunged into the city's perennial nightmare of a subterranean bloodbath. The city center was paralyzed. Police in yellow slickers sealed off streets. Bus services halted and the entire subway network closed down as rescue workers and paramedics went deep below ground to look for the dead and wounded. Above ground, an explosion tore open the roof of a No. 30 double-decker bus with such force that it threw debris 10 feet into the air. The blast was so powerful that, hours later, the police could not estimate the number of dead. Neither, said Deputy Assistant Commissioner Brian Paddick, was it clear whether the explosions were suicide bombings.*

# Fri 08-Jul-05 09:35

*Read Acts 5*

Acts 5:38-39
*³⁸And now I say unto you, Refrain from these men, and let them alone: for if this counsel or this work be of men, it will come to nought:*
*³⁹But if it be of God, ye cannot overthrow it; lest haply ye be found even to fight against God.*

This Pharisee made a very wise statement. He could have said, "The proof is in the pudding." He said if what these disciples of Jesus said is false then they will disperse and with them will go their belief, but if it is true then the Jewish leaders will be fighting against God.. So many people question the Christian faith. They say that it is a hoax. They say that Jesus really didn't rise from the dead, or possibly never died. If this was the case, then his disciples, who were mere men, would have never put their lives on the line for the case of the cross. Almost all of the disciples were martyred for their faith. As history has progressed there have been many martyrs. Many of whom died for their faith. What would you do for the cause of Christ? Would you face imprisonment? Would you die for your faith? Is your faith in Christ strong enough? Jesus calls for us all to trust in Him. He will strengthen our faith and carry us through.

NEWS OF THE DAY
Fri 08-Jul-05

*BAGHDAD, Iraq -- More than 40 people have died and some 100 have been wounded in bomb attacks on Shia pilgrims converging on a shrine in northern Baghdad, say police. At least 30 died when a suicide bomber targeted a crowd walking through the predominantly Sunni Adhamiya district to the Imam Moussa al-Kadhim mosque. Eleven pilgrims were killed in other bombings across the capital. Security had been stepped up to protect the thousands of pilgrims attending a festival that culminates on Thursday.*

## Sun 10-Jul-05 10:08

Acts 9:20-22
*[20]And straightway he preached Christ in the synagogues, that he is the Son of God.*

*[21]But all that heard him were amazed, and said; Is not this he that destroyed them which called on this name in Jerusalem, and came hither for that intent, that he might bring them bound unto the chief priests?*

*[22]But Saul increased the more in strength, and confounded the Jews which dwelt at Damascus, proving that this is very Christ.*

Abraham Lincoln used to preach to the corn in the fields as a child. My younger brother used to preach to the stuffed animals in his bedroom. What have you done to show your faith? It doesn't have to be preaching. What Jesus wants is for us to be willing to serve Him. There should be a visual change in our life. The proof is in the pudding. If you are a believer then others will see you as a follower of

Christ. There won't be any question. Christ will be evident in your life. Our desire should be that others see Christ through us.

**Thought for the day:** How do other people see me? Do they see Jesus in me?

---

NEWS OF THE DAY
Sun 10-Jul-05

*BAGHDAD -- Bombs in three Iraqi cities killed 30 people and wounded about 75, authorities said Sunday. In Baghdad, a suicide bomber killed 22 people, including five Iraqi police officers, and wounded more than 50 others at an Iraqi army recruiting center, Iraqi security sources said.*
*The blast occurred about 8:55 a.m., police said, when a bomber wearing an explosives vest underneath his clothing detonated among recruits.*
*Recruiting centers are a frequent target for insurgents in Iraq. Last weekend, an attack targeted a Baghdad army brigade headquarters.*

# Mon 11-Jul-05 09:54

Acts 9:13-17

*[13]Then Ananias answered, Lord, I have heard by many of this man, how much evil he hath done to thy saints at Jerusalem:*

*[14]And here he hath authority from the chief priests to bind all that call on thy name.*

*[15]But the Lord said unto him, Go thy way: for he is a chosen vessel unto me, to bear my name before the Gentiles, and kings, and the children of Israel:*

*[16]For I will shew him how great things he must suffer for my name's sake.*

*[17]And Ananias went his way, and entered into the house; and putting his hands on him said, Brother Saul, the Lord, even Jesus, that appeared unto thee in the way as thou camest, hath sent me, that thou mightest receive thy sight, and be filled with the Holy Ghost.*

Recently I have been feeling a little oppressed. There have been times when I really feel that these words are falling on deaf ears. I mean why should I have anything to say? I am just a man trying to understand what is in God's word. Why would anyone else want to see what I am learning? As I was reading today's word, God spoke to me and let me understand that He wanted me to write this. It is not an act of my will but of His. So many times we look at our circumstances and think that they are not what we want. We try to figure out why and all we hear is God telling us to stay the course. He is not finished with us yet. Ananias, was told by God to go and see Saul. His first inclination was to question God. He said, "Don't you know that this the man who has the ability to kill us Christians." God's message was to just do what I told you. I will use you to tell him who I am. Are we willing to allow God to use us?

Lord, use me today and forgive my unbelieving heart.

---

NEWS OF THE DAY
Mon 11-Jul-05

*BAGHDAD, Iraq -- Suspected insurgents attacked an Iraqi army checkpoint north of Baghdad on Monday, killing seven soldiers, police said. The attack left two other soldiers and three civilians wounded, police said. It occurred at the southern entrance to Khales, a town about 37 miles (60 kilometers) north of Baghdad. U.S. and Iraqi forces are conducting operations east of Khales in Buhriz. They've detained at least 30 suspected insurgents. Elsewhere, U.S. soldiers detained 13 people on Sunday and Monday on suspicion of making and placing roadside bombs in north-central Iraq, the military said Monday.*

# Tue 12-Jul-05 10:09

3 John 1:3-4
*For I rejoiced greatly, when the brethren came and testified of the truth that is in thee, even as thou walkest in the truth.*

*I have no greater joy than to hear that my children walk in truth.*

Eulogies are a time when people get to tell of what you have done during your life. You hear about how great people were. A couple of years I went to my Uncle Ed's funeral. As I sat there listening to all the different people who had been touched by him, I thought about how great this man was. He was a scientist and had worked for NASA. He had designed a machine that was used to cut Cataracts off of people's eyes. He was extremely smart. What amazed me though, was how none of the eulogies were about these things that had done. Instead they were about what a man of God he was. There were stories of how he was always willing to use his God given talents to help others. I am sure that God was rejoicing as he heard every one testifying to Ed Baehr's life. I imagine that as Uncle Ed was standing there with Jesus, that Jesus told him, "Well done thou good and faithful servant." What an amazing thought.

As I was reading this verse, I began to wonder, "What type of testimony will I leave behind?" I have the job that I do, but can others see the truth in me. When it is my time to leave this world will others give God glory for the truth they saw in me? My ultimate desire is to hear God telling me well done. Will you hear that from him? Is that your desire? May it be so, today.

---

NEWS OF THE DAY
Tue 12-Jul-05

*WASHINGTON D.C., USA -- The number of Americans who believe the war in Iraq has made the United States less safe from terrorism spiked sharply after last week's terror attacks in London, according to the latest CNN/USA Today/Gallup poll. President Bush's approval rating, meanwhile, edged up slightly, according to the poll of 1,006 Americans conducted Thursday through Sunday. The poll shows the president's approval rating rose to 49 percent -- up 3 percentage points from a poll taken June 29-30. That change was within the poll's margin of error of plus or minus 3 percentage points. Just over two weeks ago, a poll taken June 24-26 showed Bush's approval rating matching his all-time low of 45 percent, first reached in a poll taken March 21-23. Addressing a crowd Monday at the FBI training academy in Virginia, Bush vowed that the United States and free countries around the world will not cower in the face of terrorism.*

# Wed 13-Jul-05 09:16

1 Peter 2:2
*As newborn babes, desire the sincere milk of the word, that ye may grow thereby:*

I remember when my son was just a baby. He was a hungry little guy. Every 4 hours my wife would have to feed him and he never would want to stop. As he has gotten older though, his eating habits changed. He eats more food but less often. Sometimes the food is not as nourishing as I would want him to eat, but at least he is eating. This is the same way it is with us as believers. We should crave the Word of God. Our desire should be that we are always meditating on it. Most believers, as time goes by begin to pick and choose what they want to read out of the Word. We must get back to realizing that God gave us the whole word for a reason. May we never get tired of reading it and meditating on it.

---

## NEWS OF THE DAY
### Wed 13-Jul-05

*BAGHDAD, Iraq -- A suicide bomber blew up a vehicle Wednesday near a U.S. military convoy and a large group of Iraqi children in Baghdad, killing 27 people, Iraqi police and hospital officials said. Iraqi police said most of the dead were children. The attack also left 20 people wounded. The U.S. military said at least seven children and a U.S. soldier died in the attack. Three U.S. soldiers were wounded. The soldiers were handing out treats to the children when the bomb went off, police said. The attack -- which happened around 10:50 a.m. (2:50 a.m. ET) in the eastern Baghdad neighborhood of al-Jaddeda -- also set a nearby house on fire, police said. "The car bomber made a deliberate decision to attack one of our vehicles as the soldiers were engaged in a peaceful operation with Iraqi citizens," Maj. Russ Goemaere said in a statement. "The terrorist undoubtedly saw the children around the Humvee as he attacked. The complete disregard for civilian life in this attack is absolutely abhorrent."*

## Thu 14-Jul-05 09:34

Psalm 66:16
*Come and hear, all ye that fear God, and I will declare what he hath done for my soul.*

"Can I get someone to testify?" Have you ever heard that in church? Very rarely do we ever actually hear what God has done for us. There might be people who tell us something that God has done for them but normally you hear, "Can you pray for this need".

My love language is hearing that I am doing a good job. I like for people to recognize the job that I have done. I imagine that God likes to hear our thanks, as well, for what He has done for us. He doesn't do things so that He will get thanked but at the same time I am sure that it means a lot to hear thank you. What has God done for you lately? I can tell you he has kept me safe and he is directing my life. He is taking care of my family while I am away. He is ever patient with me through my spiritual and physical struggles. He is a forgiving father. I am grateful to have Him as my Lord. What has he done for you? Tell someone, today.

---

NEWS OF THE DAY
Thu 14-Jul-05

*BAGHDAD, Iraq -- U.S.-led coalition forces have captured two alleged leaders of the insurgent group al Qaeda in Iraq, including a man suspected in the death of an Egyptian envoy, an American military spokesman said Thursday. Troops caught Khamis Farhan Khalaf abd al Fahdawi, also known as Abu Seba, on Saturday in Ramadi, west of Baghdad, after intelligence led them there. Abu Seba reportedly is a senior lieutenant for`Jordanian-born militant Abu Musab al-Zarqawi and is suspected in this month's attacks on Bahraini and Pakistani diplomats and the killing of Ihab al-Sherif, who came to Iraq to be Egypt's ambassador. Al-Sherif was kidnapped in Baghdad on July 2, and the Egyptian government confirmed his death five days later. In addition, forces detained Abdulla Ibrahim Muhammed Hassan al Shadad, also known as Abu Abdul Aziz, on Sunday in Baghdad. He reportedly is the leader of al-Zarqawi's operations in the Iraqi capital and a key officer for the insurgent group.*

## Fri 15-Jul-05 09:43

I Thessalonians 4:14-17
*¹⁴For if we believe that Jesus died and rose again, even so them also which sleep in Jesus will God bring with him.*
*¹⁵For this we say unto you by the word of the Lord, that we which are alive and remain unto the coming of the Lord shall not prevent them which are asleep.*

*<sup>16</sup>For the Lord himself shall descend from heaven with a shout, with the voice of the archangel, and with the trump of God: and the dead in Christ shall rise first:*

*<sup>17</sup>Then we which are alive and remain shall be caught up together with them in the clouds, to meet the Lord in the air: and so shall we ever be with the Lord.*

I once heard a story of a young man who was attending a small Christian College. He was so excited about the coming of the Lord, that it was all he could talk about. One day he awoke to a loud trumpet sound that was blasting all over campus. He exclaimed, "The Lord is coming back!" But then he began to look around and realized that he was the only one around. Everyone else was gone. He began to worry and wonder if his faith had been strong enough. Then his friends came out of hiding. This was a pretty cruel prank but it does make a good point. We don't when Christ will come back. All we know is how He will be announced. The Day of the Lord will come with the sound of a trumpet. It will be just like a king who is coming out to see his commoners and the trumpeters would announce his presence.

This is exactly what will happen when Christ comes back. The only difference is that Christ will call for all of us to come up to him. All of those believers who have died will rise to meet Christ in the air. Then those who believe will arise to meet Him. That will be the beginning of eternity for us. What a wonderful thought. What is comforting to me is that Christ is raising us to His standard. Most kings remain at their level and the commoners stay where they are, but Jesus loves us enough that He wants us to be with Him. What an awesome privilege!

---

## NEWS OF THE DAY
### Fri 15-Jul-05

*BAGHDAD, Iraq -- The recent surge in jihadist activity was exemplified on July 15 by multiple suicide attacks targeting the U.S.-led coalition, Iraqi security forces, and Iraqi government targets in Baghdad. The Surge, while following the established pattern of jihadist operational activity, demonstrates that U.S. and Iraqi efforts to pacify the capital have been unsuccessful. The U.S.*

*and Iraqi authorities will likely conduct an operation within the next few days to root out the resurgent jihadist cells. As U.S.-led coalition and Iraqi forces sweep through Baghdad, they will encounter resistance by nationalist and jihadist insurgents as their base areas are penetrated. This resistance will be characterized by battles featuring direct fire from small arms and rocket-propelled grenades (RPGs). Similarly, As Samarra has been the scene of frequent clashes between insurgents and U.S.-led coalition and Iraqi forces. The reported fighting in the town on the Tigris river on July 15 comes two weeks after a similar raid.*

## Sun 17-Jul-05 11:04

Matthew 13:24-30

*²⁴Another parable put he forth unto them, saying, The kingdom of heaven is likened unto a man which sowed good seed in his field:*

*²⁵But while men slept, his enemy came and sowed tares among the wheat, and went his way.*

*²⁶But when the blade was sprung up, and brought forth fruit, then appeared the tares also.*

*²⁷So the servants of the householder came and said unto him, Sir, didst not thou sow good seed in thy field? from whence then hath it tares?*

*²⁸He said unto them, An enemy hath done this. The servants said unto him, Wilt thou then that we go and gather them up?*

*²⁹But he said, Nay; lest while ye gather up the tares, ye root up also the wheat with them.*

*³⁰Let both grow together until the harvest: and in the time of harvest I will say to the reapers, Gather ye together first the tares, and bind them in bundles to burn them: but gather the wheat into my barn.*

Today in our worship service the Chaplain used these verses to take his message from. I had never really thought about what these verses meant. I understood that believers were the wheat and that non-believers were the weeds, but I didn't ever grasp the meaning beyond that. The impression that I have now gotten is that we are never going to be able to pull out the weeds. We will never win the war against good and evil. Notice I said "we". It is not my job to fight the evil that is around me. Life will not be fair. People will always try to knock you down or step on you to get to the top.

Instead, we must realize that the judgment day is coming. The master will have all of the fields cut down. Once that happens then the wheat and the weeds will be separated. The believers and the non-believers will be separated. At that time we will be given the reward that is due. The most important thing is knowing that we are wheat. We must take comfort in knowing we are named after Christ. Take joy in that today.

## NEWS OF THE DAY
Sun 17-Jul-05

*WASHINGTON D.C., USA -- In the months before the Iraqi elections in January, President Bush approved a plan to provide covert support to certain Iraqi candidates and political parties, but rescinded the proposal because of Congressional opposition, current and former government officials said Saturday. In a statement issued in response to questions about a report in the next issue of The New Yorker, Frederick Jones, the spokesman for the National Security Council, said that "in the final analysis, the president determined and the United States government adopted a policy that we would not try -- and did not try -- to influence the outcome of the Iraqi election by covertly helping individual candidates for office." The statement appeared to leave open the question of whether any covert help was provided to parties favored by Washington, an issue about which the White House declined to elaborate.*

# Tue 19-Jul-05 08:49

Romans 3:9-10
*What then? Are we better than they? No, in no wise: for we have before proved both Jews and Gentiles, that they are all under sin; As it is written, there is none righteous, no, not one.*

Recently, I have become convicted that sometimes I tend to look down my nose at people. I think that I am better than they are. "I would never act like that" is something that would flash through my mind. I have taken a step outside of my life in Christ and stepped into the worldly self. You see, Christ didn't ever say, "I am better than they are." He would associate with the lowest of low. He would try to lead them to the light. His attitude though, was that of humility. Jesus had every right to say that He was better than us. He was perfect. All of us are sinners. We don't have that right to act or think that we are better than anyone else. Lord, Make me humble and use me to lead others to you.

---

### NEWS OF THE DAY
Tue 19-Jul-05

*BAQUBAH, Iraq -- Gunmen in two cars opened fire on a minibus full of Iraqis traveling to work at a U.S. base today, killing eight of them and injuring the driver, officials said. The attack took place about three miles north of Baqubah on the road to Khalis. A relative of one of the victims confirmed that the Iraqis worked at the American base in Khalis. On Monday, at least 25 police, soldiers and government workers were slain in a series of ambushes and shootings, officials said. The deadliest attack was in the western Baghdad district of Khadra, where eight policemen died in a gun battle with insurgents, police said. Gunmen also killed at least five other police officers, including a colonel, in attacks around the capitol, police and hospital officials said. Three civilian government employees were killed in separate ambushes in Baghdad, police reported.*

## Fri 22-Jul-05 09:31

1 Peter 2:12
*Having your conversations honest among the Gentiles: that, whereas they speak against you as evildoers, they may by your good works, which they shall behold, glorify God in the day of visitation.*

Recently I was sitting in a meeting where we were talking about this very thing. There were people who had been speaking nasty rumors about certain individuals. The person whose name was being drug through the mud was expressing their feelings about the whole thing. Sometimes when we hear something told to us about someone else our immediate inclination is to tell someone else. As a believer, we are encouraged to keep our conversations honest. The really interesting thing about this is that Peter writes that we should keep our conversations honest (or true) among the Gentiles. It is

much easier to keep your mouth pure when you are among
Christians, but when you are among non-believers the temptation is
to talk like they talk. When we do this, we are portraying a bad image
of Christ to those around us. We must decide what type of image we
want to portray to others. Do we want them to see Christ or
someone else? Let us portray Christ in everything we do and SAY.

---

NEWS OF THE DAY
Fri 22-Jul-05

*MANILA, Philippines -- A Filipino citizen taken hostage in Iraq almost eight
months ago has been released from captivity, Philippines President Gloria
Macapagal Arroyo has said. "Robert Tarongoy is finally coming home," Arroyo
said in a written statement released to the news media Wednesday. "Robert is
now safe in the hands of the Iraq hostage crisis team led by Undersecretary
Rafael Seguis who is making the necessary arrangements to bring him back to
the Philippines," Arroyo said. "Ivy Tarongoy, Robert's wife, told me she is
overjoyed and deeply grateful for this good news." Tarongoy was abducted by
militants on November 1, 2004, from a villa in Baghdad owned by the Saudi
company that employed him as an accountant. Four of the workers were quickly
freed, but the militant group is still believed to be holding American Roy
Hallums.
The Philippines government, whose diplomatic team in Iraq has been talking
to the captors through mediators, said in March the abductors had indefinitely
extended a deadline for Tarongoy's execution.*

# Sat 23-Jul-05 10:16

Hebrews 8:12
*For I will be merciful to their unrighteousness, and their sins
and their iniquities will I remember no more.*

What a God we serve! Here is our heavenly father, who
initially created man to be able to commune with him. God didn't
create us so that He could have dominion over us. He wanted us to
talk with and live with him in unity. When man sinned, all of that
was destroyed. There was a great divide. Man couldn't get to God
anymore. God didn't want that divide there, so He put in place a
plan to bridge the great divide. He sent Jesus to take mans place and

die for our sin. Because of Christ, God says that He will remember man's sin no more.

What did I ever do to deserve this type of love? We truly serve an awesome God. If you don't know about this love that He has for you, may you seek to find Him today.

---

*BAGHDAD, Iraq -- Marine Sgt. Bryan J. Opskar (32) died July 23, 2005 Serving During Operation Iraqi Freedom. He was assigned to the 2nd Light Armored Reconnaissance Battalion, 2nd Marine Division, II Marine Expeditionary Force, Camp Lejeune, N.C. and was killed July 23 when his vehicle was struck by an improvised explosive device while he was conducting combat operations near Rutbah, Iraq.*

## Sun 24-Jul-05 10:33

2 Corinthians 9:15
*Thanks be unto God for his unspeakable gift.*

What has God given to you? Has He given you health? Has He given you friendships? Has He provided for you financially so that you have no needs? How many times do we take the time to praise God? Sitting here in Iraq, I am impressed even more of what God is doing for us. I live in a country where I am allowed to worship my God. I don't have to worry about what type of repercussions there might be if I am caught going to church. I am taken care of financially. I have a wonderful family. I am blessed to be alive. God is truly great. We must be able to speak the gifts that God has given us. Sometimes though we need to just thank Him for what we can't speak. He understands.

**Thought for the day:** What has God done for you? Have you thanked HIM?

---

*BAGHDAD, Iraq -- Four National Guard Soldiers died while they were on patrol when an improvised explosive device detonated near their HMMWV in Baghdad, Iraq on July 24. The Soldiers were supporting Operation Iraqi Freedom. The Soldiers were assigned to Company A, 2nd Battalion, 121st Infantry Regiment, 48th Infantry Brigade, 24th Infantry Division. Dead are:*

- *Spc. Jacques E. Brunson, 30, of Americus, Ga. He was an infantryman.*
- *Staff. Sgt. Carl. R. Fuller, 44, of Covington, Ga. He was an infantryman.*
- *Sgt. James O. Kinlow, 35, of Thomson, Ga. He was a cannon crewmember.*
- *Sgt. John F. Thomas, 33, of Valdosta, Ga. He was an infantryman.*

*All four Soldiers deployed to Iraq in May 2005. The 48th Brigade is one of three National Guard enhanced Separate Brigades that fall under the command of the 24th Infantry Division (Mech).*

## Tue 26-Jul-05 08:21

1 Thessalonians 5:12-13
*¹²And we beseech you, brethren, to know them which labour among you, and are over you in the Lord, and admonish you;*
*¹³And to esteem them very highly in love for their work's sake. And be at peace among yourselves.*

I am the type of person that will lose my cool in a heartbeat. A couple of weeks ago someone was talking to me about some things that I had done. This person was in a position of authority, but the way that I was talking to him was as a peer. When he started to question me and what I have been doing I went on the defensive. I said some things that I probably shouldn't have said. I had to go to him later and apologize. There are times when we just don't want to be corrected. We can't stand to have anyone else tell us that we are wrong. The verse today says that we should know those that are placed in positions of authority over us. It doesn't mean that we have to flatter them so that we can be on their good side. What this is saying is that we should know them and that we need to lift them up in prayer. The scripture continues that they are over us in

219

the Lord. These are believers who are in the church. So many times we go to church to "feel good" and if we get our toes stepped on we leave because the church didn't make us feel good. We are to lift up those in authority in church as well. Our pastors, deacons, and Sunday school teachers all need to be lifted up. They are going about God's work. Because they are going about God's work they are more liable to be attacked by Satan. We must not forget to lift them up and pray for them daily so that the enemy may be kept away.

---

NEWS OF THE DAY
Tue 26-Jul-05

*BAGHDAD, Iraq -- Sunni Arab leaders who suspended participation in drafting Iraq's new constitution after one of their negotiators was assassinated made clear Monday that they would return to the talks, most likely today, after receiving assurances from Iraqi and U.S. officials.*

*"We have decided to rejoin," said Iyad Samarrai, a member of the Sunni delegation and a senior figure in the Iraqi Islamic Party.*
*The Sunni delegates left the talks last week after one of their negotiators, Mijbil Issa, was assassinated along with a legal advisor to the delegation and a friend. Although the assassination was the precipitating factor, Sunnis had also expressed unease with the reluctance of Kurds and Shiites to take Sunni positions seriously. Key to their return was the assurance that the government would pay for security guards for Sunni delegates, as it does for members of the National Assembly, even though the Sunni delegates are not elected Assembly members.*

# Wed 27-Jul-05 09:00

Acts 12:5
*Peter therefore was kept in prison: but prayer was made without ceasing of the church unto God for him.*

I have never really been good at numbers and math but I want to try to do some calculations for a minute. When I left for Iraq, there were probably 50 people who committed to pray for me and my unit while I was deployed. Now if those people prayed for us once a day the whole time that we were deployed then that would have been 18250 prayers during the whole year. If they had prayed twice a day for us then it would have been 36500 prayers issued on our behalf. Now imagine, just for a minute, that each of those people asked just two people as well to pray for us and they all committed to praying three times a day. 164250 prayers would have been lifted up for us. I know that these numbers are small compared to the number of people that are praying for us daily but it shows just how many prayers would have been lifted up to our heavenly Father for us.

To many of us Iraq seems to be a prison for us. We are away from our families and other loved ones. We must be reminded that there are many people that are praying for our safe return. We must also remember that we must pray for others as well. Prayer does change things. Let us remember this today.

**Challenge:** Read the rest of Acts 12 and see how the prayers of the church changed Peter's life.

---

## NEWS OF THE DAY
Wed 27-Jul-05

*FALLUJAH, Iraq -- Matthew Higginbotham is one of many Marines who spend their days staring out at vast expanses of wasteland and urban ruins. He peers out at the desolation through a rifle-mounted scope, with only a thin covering of camouflage netting to provide him shade from the summer's blistering Iraqi sun. "I feel like I'm in hell right now, because it's so hot out here," stated the 19-year old infantryman from Greenup, Ky. "You're sweating constantly, especially your feet, because you're wearing boots all the time, sometimes almost 24 hours a day."*

*As the mid-July temperatures reach 120 degrees Fahrenheit, the 2004 Greenup County High School graduate's unit has not relented in continuing their efforts to rid Fallujah of a persistent insurgency. If anything, Higginbotham's unit, Company C, 1st Battalion, 6th Marine Regiment, has raised its operational tempo right beside their thermometer's mercury level. Since arriving here in mid-March, Higginbotham and the Marines from the unit has operated alongside Iraqi Security Forces to conduct continuous patrols, raids and humanitarian missions throughout the once-embattled city.*

*"We do patrols for three days, stand guard posts for three days, and go out to work with the Iraqi soldiers to help them out and teach them things," stated*

*Higginbotham, describing his typical work week. He spends much of his time
here serving sentry duty in various posts around Company C's base of
operations, an abandoned train station outside northern Fallujah.*

## Fri 29-Jul-05 09:38

*Read Judges 3*

Judges 3:9, 15
*And when the children of Israel cried unto the Lord, the Lord
raised up a deliverer to the children of Israel, who delivered them, even
Othniel the son of Kenaz, Caleb's younger brother.*
*But when the children of Israel cried unto the Lord, the Lord
raised them up a deliverer, Ehud the son of Gera, a Benjamite, a man
lefthanded: and by him the children of Israel sent a present unto Eglon
the king of Moab.*

I am the oldest of eleven children. When we were younger
there were times that we would get into arguments or fights and my
parents would have to intervene and fix the problem. This is what
God had to do for the Israelites. If you read the book of Judges you
should see a trend. The Israelites would be delivered by God. Then
there would be a time of peace. Then Israel would sin. After the sin
there would be suffering and they would have to serve a foreign
nation. Then they would cry out to God. (Scofield Bible
Commentary for Judges 3:7) It was a vicious cycle.

As I was reading this I began to wonder how this applies to
us today. There is a cycle in our life as well. We call them mountain
tops and valleys. It is probably the same thing. We are on a spiritual
high. Then we sin and we fall into a valley. Then we cry out to God
to forgive us and He helps bring us out of our pit. We live for a while
on a spiritual high but then we falter again. Why does it take falling
away from God to bring us back to Him? Why can't we stay on that
mountain top? The answers to these questions are twofold. First of
all if we remain on the mountain top we will become stagnant and
we will not grow. We will think that we are self sufficient. Secondly,
man is sinful. No matter how hard we try to not sin, we will sin and
fall away from God. We must rely on Him to bring us out of the
depths of despair. The one positive thing in all of this is that we can

222

control how far we slip and how long we stay in the valley. If our relationship with God is a close one, we will see that we are starting to slip. We will call out to Him for help and forgiveness, rather than waiting until we have totally fallen. The goal should be to stay out of the valley. Let God help do that today.

   **Thought for the day**: Where are you now? Are you on the mountain top, in the valley or somewhere in between?

---

### NEWS OF THE DAY
Fri 29-Jul-05

*BAGHDAD, Iraq -- A suicide bomber killed at least 26 people on Friday in an attack on an army recruiting center in the northern Iraqi town of Rubia, police told CNN. The bomber blew himself up among a group of recruits, police said. At least 30 people were wounded, police said.*
*Rubia is near the Syrian border, and the spokesman said that authorities temporarily closed border crossings after the attack. Iraqi police and army facilities have been a frequent target of insurgent attacks.*

*On Thursday, two Marines were killed when insurgents fired small arms and rocket-propelled grenades at their unit during combat operations in Cykla, the U.S. military said in a statement issued on Friday.*

*Cykla, located in Anbar province about 120 miles west of Baghdad, is the same village where Marines launched an airstrike Thursday against insurgents after they and Iraqi forces were ambushed while on patrol.Nine insurgents, including five identified as Syrians, were killed in the clash. The military did not say whether the two Marines were killed in the same incident.*

## Sun 31-Jul-05 10:38

1 Thessalonians 1:6
*For ye became followers of us, and of the Lord, having received the word in much affliction, with joy of the Holy Ghost:*

How will they know Christ? This is a question that I have asked myself over the years. As a young teenager, I conducted a small Child Evangelism Fellowship meeting at my house with my brother. We had about 10-12 kids come to it every week for four to six weeks.

They would learn about the Bible and about Jesus, as well as play games and such. The last year that we conducted it we had a celebration cookout on the last day. All of us kids were wrestling around. As some of the kids were trying to tackle me I threw one kid off of my back, breaking his collarbone. When confronted by it though, I adamantly denied doing it. I blamed it on one of the other kids. I finally ended up telling the truth, but it took a lot of prodding. Was this the way that Christ wanted me to act? Is this the way that Christ should be represented? What type of light was I being? My actions were much louder than words. Here I was telling the kids about Jesus and how He wanted us to live, but then when I was put in a compromising situation I turned the light off and my true self shone through. The light must shine through no matter what the consequences.

Paul's message was that the people became followers of the disciples first. Then they became followers of Christ. We are a representation of Christ. People will come to Him because of us. If we are living in the world and acting like the world then we will not look any different than what the world is. Jesus wants us to be a representation of Him. Jesus calls us a light. He wants us to draw men unto him. If we are the light then we will lead others to him. Let us be a light for others to follow, today.

---

NEWS OF THE DAY
Sun 31-Jul-05

*BAGHDAD, Iraq -- Iraqi troops of the Second Brigade-Desert Lion kiss the Iraq national flag before raising it during the Iskanian military base handover ceremony, July 31, 2005, in Baqubah, 40 miles north of Baghdad, Iraq. The base was handed over to the Iraqi forces by the U.S. military who have held it since the fall of Iraq's military under Saddam Hussein's regime two years ago.*

# Mon 01-Aug-05 09:52

Romans 5:3-5
*³And not only so, but we glory in tribulations also: knowing that tribulation worketh patience;*

224

*⁴And patience, experience; and experience, hope:*
*⁵And hope maketh not ashamed; because the love of God is*
*shed abroad in our hearts by the Holy Ghost which is given unto us.*

I was talking to my wife this morning and she told me about what the pastor in my home church was talking about during yesterday's service. He was talking about when you have tribulation and the places that we need to look. He said that we shouldn't look or dwell in your circumstances. Instead we need to remember what God has done for us in the past. We must look around us and seek help from other believers. We must look up, to God for help as well.

Paul gives three solutions for tribulation as well. First of all he says that it brings patience. Secondly he says that it brings experience. Thirdly it brings us hope. Tribulations will come. You can't prevent them. Since there are always going to be tribulations then we must be able take something from it. If we allow it we can gain patience through the tribulation. Once we have been able to become patient we should be able to learn something from the problem. If we learn something, then we can utilize that experience in the future when other issues happen. Our experience should bring hope. Do you have something that is troubling you? First, give it to God so that he can give you the patience to experience the hope that we have in Christ.

---

## NEWS OF THE DAY
### Mon 01-Aug-05

*BAGHDAD, Iraq -- 6 Marine Snipers Are Slain in Ambush in Western Iraq. The Americans said the six marines killed Monday afternoon had formed a pair of sniper teams that were working near Haditha, one of a string of cities along the Euphrates River believed to make up the main infiltration route for guerrillas entering Iraq and moving toward Baghdad. The snipers were working in two teams of three men each; both teams were wiped out.*

*"I don't believe there are any surviving eyewitnesses," a senior Marine officer said, speaking on condition of anonymity. The ambush follows at least a half-dozen American military offensives in the area to root out insurgents and shut down the "rat line," as it is called, that is believed to shuttle insurgents from sanctuaries on or across the Syrian border into the Iraqi heartland. The*

*Americans staged the operations in the hope of restoring Iraqi authority, but the guerrillas have proved resilient.*

*Ansar al Sunna, an insurgent group, took responsibility for the ambush in a posting on an Islamist Web site, claiming that its men, which it called the Lions of Monotheism, had killed eight marines, "some of them by guns and others by beheading."*

## Thu 04-Aug-05 09:15

Ecclesiastes 3:1-8
*[1]To everything there is a season, and a time to every purpose under the heaven:*
*[2]A time to be born, and a time to die; a time to plant, and a time to pluck up that which is planted;*
*[3]A time to kill, and a time to heal; a time to break down, and a time to build up;*
*[4]A time to weep, and a time to laugh; a time to mourn, and a time to dance;*
*[5]A time to cast away stones, and a time to gather stones together; a time to embrace, and a time to refrain from embracing;*
*[6]A time to get, and a time to lose; a time to keep, and a time to cast away;*
*[7]A time to rend, and a time to sew; a time to keep silence, and a time to speak;*
*[8]A time to love, and a time to hate; a time of war, and a time of peace.*

**For everything there is a season**... Those words are so powerful. I have seen seasons come and I have seen them go here in Iraq. Well I really don't know if you can call them seasons. It was winter then it was summer. Anyway, I have learned a lot during this time though. God has really shown me many things that I have needed to see, as well.

When I first started writing the Word of the day/Word from a Soldier, I never thought that it would amount to anything big. In August of 2004 I received an email with a thought provoking message for the day. In response to that email I felt God lead me to respond to the sender with a scriptural "Word for the Day". This sparked the daily devotionals that you started receiving through your email. Each devotional was written from the heart and I have felt that God was showing me where I needed to work in my life as I would write them. No longer was I writing these devotionals for just a few people. My distribution lists have grown quite large and I have also heard where other people forward it to others.

Now, one year later, I feel that it is time for me to conclude writing these devotionals. I have enjoyed writing them, but I feel that it is time to put up my keyboard and seek God's face as to what He wants me to do next. The time has been precious. I really appreciate all of the words of encouragement that you have sent my way.

Please pray for me as I seek to honor Him in what I do.
May God Richly Bless you!

---

## NEWS OF THE DAY
### Mon 04-Aug-05

*BAGHDAD, Iraq -- Another American Marine was killed in action in a city in the Euphrates River valley where 14 U.S. Marines died in the deadliest roadside bombing suffered by U.S. forces in the Iraq war, the U.S. military said. At least nine Iraqi security personnel were also killed in scattered attacks Thursday, including a car bombing which targeted members of a radical Shiite militia visiting a religious shrine.*

*The latest Marine casualty was reported from Ramadi, the capital of explosive Anbar province 70 miles west. The Marine, whose name was not released, was killed by small arms fire Wednesday — the same day that 14 Marines and an Iraqi civilian translator died in a huge bombing near Haditha. That brought to at least 24 the number of Marines killed over the last week in along the Euphrates Valley in one of the bloodiest periods for U.S. forces in months. In all, at least 45 American service members have died in Iraq since July 24 — all but two in combat.*

# -FIELD NOTES-
*for Journaling*

## About the Author

*Eric E. Scheidt, Sr. is a former Soldier who served in the United States Army from 1994 to 2012 with the 82nd Airborne Division, 67th Signal Battalion, 2nd Infantry Division, 327th Signal Battalion and in several special duty assignments that included serving on a Military Transition Team (MiTT) in support of Operation New Dawn.*

*He deployed to Afghanistan in 2003 and twice to Iraq (2004/2008). During his first deployment to Iraq, he was given the opportunity to serve as a Spiritual Lay leader for his unit. He mentored and counseled a countless number of Soldiers who needed assistance and advice. It was while he was serving in this capacity that he began writing Word from a Soldier.*

*Eric was medically discharged while serving with the 101st Airborne Division. He is married to his wife, Michelle, and currently lives near Nashville, Tennessee.*

21 Days to
**align your mind**

Eric Nichols

*www.alignyourmind.com*

RALPH "MALACHIAS" GASKIN

# A WARRIOR'S GARDEN
## SEEDS OF A THERAPEUTIC APPROACH TO DEALING WITH POST-TRAUMATIC STRESS DISORDER (PTSD)

A TRAITMARKER
BOOK CLUB
PUBLICATION

*www.awarriorsgarden.com*

| From the Library of: | |
|---|---|
| **Author:** | |
| **Title:** | |

| Date | Issued To: |
|---|---|
| | |
| | |
| | |
| | |
| | |
| | |
| | |
| | |
| | |
| | |
| | |
| | |
| | |
| | |

*Pass it on!*

Made in the USA
Columbia, SC
06 June 2023

17443137R00135